# 88
# EVANGELISTIC
# SERMONS

# 88 EVANGELISTIC SERMONS

*Edited by*

## CHARLES L. WALLIS

*Introduction by*

## CHARLES L. ALLEN

**HARPER & ROW, PUBLISHERS**

NEW YORK, EVANSTON,

AND LONDON

# Acknowledgments

Special acknowledgment is made to the following who have granted permission for the reprinting of copyrighted material from the books listed below:

ABINGDON PRESS for extracts from *Sermons from Revelation* by Clovis G. Chappell, copyright 1943 by Whitmore & Stone; *The Greatest Questions of the Bible and of Life* by Clarence Edward Macartney, copyright 1948 by Stone & Pierce; *Not a Sparrow Falls* by Paul Quillian, copyright 1952 by Pierce & Washabaugh; *Rediscovering the Words of Faith* by Charles T. Sardeson, copyright © 1956 by Pierce & Washabaugh.

CHANNEL PRESS for extract from sermon by W. E. Sangster in *Evangelical Sermons of Our Day*, ed. by Andrew W. Blackwood, copyright © 1959.

DOULEDAY & COMPANY for extract from *The Secret of Happiness* by Billy Graham, copyright © 1955 by Billy Graham.

WM. B. EERDMANS PUBLISHING COMPANY for extracts from *The Cross through the Open Tomb* by Donald Grey Barnhouse, copyright © 1961; *Beneath the Cross of Jesus* by Reginald E. O. White, copyright © 1959.

HARPER & ROW for extracts from *No Escape from Life* by John Sutherland Bonnell, copyright © 1958; *Favorite Sermons of John A. Broadus*, ed. by V. L. Stanfield, copyright © 1959; *From Skepticism to Faith* by Charles Fiske, copyright 1934; *The Best of John A. Hutton*, copyright 1950; *The Best of Alexander Maclaren*, copyright 1949; *The Face of God* by G. Stanley Russell, copyright 1935; *Life at Its Best* by Avery Albert Shaw, copyright 1934; *National Awakening* by Samuel M. Shoemaker, copyright 1936; *The Best of Studdert-Kennedy*, copyright 1948, reprinted by permission of Harper & Row and Hodder & Stoughton; *Our Common Loyalty* by Philemon G. Sturges, copyright 1936; *Christ and the Meaning of Life* by Helmut Thielicke, copyright © 1962, reprinted by permission of Harper & Row and James Clarke & Company.

HODDER & STOUGHTON for extracts from *The Day of the Cross* by W. M. Clow; *The Way Everlasting* by James Denney; *The Gateways of the Stars* by George H. Morrison.

McCLELLAND & STEWART for extract from *Rainbows through the Rain* by W. A. Cameron.

FLEMING H. REVELL COMPANY for extracts from *The Silences of Jesus* by Percy Ainsworth; *The Gift of Influence* by Hugh Black; sermon by W. A. Criswell in *The Pulpit in the South*, ed. by Frank S. Mead, copyright 1950; *The Kingdom is Yours* by Louis H. Evans, copyright 1952; *The Treasury of Quiet Talks* by S. D. Gordon; *Who Goes There?* by J. Wallace Hamilton, copyright © 1958; *Difficult Sayings of Jesus* by Gordon Powell, copyright © 1962; *The Salty Tang* by Frederick B. Speakman, copyright © 1954.

CHARLES SCRIBNER'S SONS for extracts from *The Healing Cross* by Herbert H. Farmer, copyright 1935, reprinted by permission of Charles Scribner's Sons and James Nisbet and Company; *The Galilean Accent* by Arthur John Gossip, copyright 1926, reprinted by permission of Charles Scribner's Sons and T. & T. Clark; *His Gifts and Promises* by James Moffatt; "O World" from *Poems* by George Santayana, copyright 1921 by George Santayana; *The Gates of New Life* by James S. Stewart, copyright 1938, reprinted by permission of Charles Scribner's Sons and T. & T. Clark.

WESTMINSTER PRESS for extract from *Design for Christian Living* by Hugh Thomson Kerr, reprinted by permission of Donald C. Kerr.

LIBRARY OF CONGRESS CATALOG CARD NUMBER: 64-14374

D-O

# CONTENTS

### IV. BORN-AGAIN MEN

### V. THE PERIL OF DELAY

### VI. WORDS OF ETERNAL LIFE

## VII. THE FELLOWSHIP OF THE REDEEMED

## VIII. OUR LIFE IN HIM

## IX. TEXTS THAT CHALLENGE

## X. THE TASK OF THE EVANGELIST

# 88
## EVANGELISTIC
## SERMONS

# Introduction: The Preacher As Evangelist
CHARLES L. ALLEN

•

One of the world's favorite literary characters is Sherlock Holmes. The stories about that great detective are read eagerly by each new generation. However, Holmes's creator, Conan Doyle, grew tired of him and wanted to give himself to the writing of better literature. To bring to an end the series of detective stories, he wrote a final chapter in which Holmes fell over a cliff and was killed. Afterward the public so clamored for more of the stories that Doyle was persuaded to write still another story in which the detective was saved from the fall by a miracle and continued his profession.

It is strange, is it not, that the author became ashamed of his best work—really the only contribution to literature he ever made—and wanted to turn from it?

Another writer, Beatrix Potter, had a similar experience. Her name is not well known, but there is hardly one among us who is not familiar with the name Peter Rabbit. As a young lady in her thirties, she wrote the delightful story of Peter Rabbit, Mopsie, Flopsie, Cotton Tail, and Mr. McGregor.

Later Beatrix, having married a rich squire, wanted to forget the famous characters which she created. She would not allow the name of Peter Rabbit to be mentioned in her presence. She felt her literary creations were beneath her dignity and station in life. It is strange that she became ashamed of the best work she ever achieved.

One remembers how Jesus sent out the seventy to preach to the people. We are even today inspired by what happened as Peter preached on the day of Pentecost. We think of John Wesley preaching on the streets and in the coal mines, and we remember the early circuit riders in America. We recall those preachers of an earlier day whose main business was to tell people of the Christ who could save. They preached for decisions. People were converted, sometimes their cups overflowed, and they even shouted.

We have come a long way in the Church of Christ since then. We have built fine buildings, educated our preachers, and brought meaningful dignity into our worship services. But as the Church has become more sophisticated, we are tempted to be ashamed of the best labors the Church has ever accomplished.

We sing and pray,

> Come, Holy Spirit, heavenly Dove,
> With all thy quick'ning pow'rs;
> Kindle a flame of sacred love
> In these cold hearts of ours.

Then at the first manifestation of the flame being kindled, we call the fire department to put it out.

Let us never forget that the greatest work the Church undertakes is to cause a sinner to be converted. Evangelism may not be the only business of the Church, but it is the main business of Christ's people.

One day the pope was showing St. Francis some of the beautiful treasures of the Church and remarked, "No longer can the Church say, 'Silver and gold have I none.'" To which the saint replied, "And neither can the Church say, 'In the name of Jesus Christ of Nazareth rise up and walk.'" Beautiful buildings, robed choirs and ministers, and cultured congregations must never stand in the way of the primary function of the Church to introduce a lost soul to him who saves.

I recall that as a boy, growing up in the mountains of North

Georgia, I enjoyed hunting chestnuts. The trees were abundant, and the nuts were delicious. After some years a blight came upon all the chestnut trees in those mountains and they died. Those trees still had access to the nourishment of the earth, but the blight destroyed them.

Two college students heard a sermon in which the preacher talked about sin. Walking back across the campus one of them said, "What is sin?" The other replied, "That is something that had to do with Adam and Eve." Adam and Eve did have the matter of sin to deal with, but no more so than man today. There are many people with a blight upon them. Our physicians' offices are crowded with people who do not "feel good," and many times it is because they are not good.

When one is afflicted by a sense of sin, guilt, and shame, he can do several things about it. (1) He can bottle it up within himself and hope it will pass away. Yet one cannot bury a live sin in a grave of forgetfulness. (2) One can talk about it to every person who will listen, but usually such talk does little good for the soul and is bad for the reputation. (3) One may feel strong enough and sufficiently capable of handling it by himself. However, as Martin Luther said, "Sin is a knot which only God can untie." (4) One may finally realize that the only real cure of sin is to have it forgiven.

The Bible teaches, "If we confess our sins, he is faithful and just to forgive us our sins" (1 John 1:9). To recognize that sin is sin, to sorrow over it, and to be willing to change and be changed are all part of confession. As a result, Christ is enabled to do his part, which is forgiveness. When Jesus Christ died on the Cross, he gave us a perfect example of sacrifice and a revelation of God's love. On the Cross, however, he did something far more—he atoned for our sins. An old gospel song asks, "What can wash away my sins?" The answer? "Nothing but the blood of Jesus."

It has been said that this generation has lost its sense of sin, yet no generation has been more conscious of the fact that something is wrong with us and that something needs to be done. But we are a conceited people, and we have been dazzled by our own accomplishments. Our attitude seems to be, "The difficult we do immediately; the impossible takes a little longer."

So we set for ourselves vast programs of self-salvation. Witness the stream of self-help books and their amazing sales during recent years. We are told to think right, to keep busy, to take a vacation, to serve our fellow man, to live a high moral life, to forgive ourselves, and to forget the past. Such programs miserably fail because they misunderstand the basic principle of wrong. Sin cannot be rightfully described as mere personal maladjustment or antisocial behavior. Sin is against God. It is as David cried, "I have sinned against the Lord" (Sam. 12:13).

Because sin is against God, only God can forgive sin. Long ago men realized that only heaven can cleanse the stains of earth. So from the beginning of recorded history, all peoples have built altars in one form or another. While many of the altar sacrifices of ancient man seem crude, even repulsive, yet there is more sense in the crudest of altars than in our naïve efforts of self-salvation.

Let us never forget that through thousands of years the altar has represented helplessness. As long as we are filled with human pride, we do not build them. Because we have conquered large areas of nature and created for ourselves a multiplicity of mechanical devices, we are reluctant to admit that we are helpless to accomplish anything, even our own soul's salvation.

The preacher, of course, does not save any person. As an evangelist he is the introducer of the sinner to Christ. The object of that introduction is what we call conversion, and conversion takes many forms. There is the experience of Paul, of Timothy, of Zacchaeus, and hosts of others—each different and yet each leading to a relationship with Christ which leads to salvation.

How does Christ save the lost? It is mysterious and it is

supernatural, yet I fear that our theological terms have often served to confuse rather than to help many sincere seekers. As one reads the Four Gospels, he sees Jesus as a very lovable person. He taught and inspired people, laughed and played with children, and loved birds and flowers. He was such a person that others liked to be near him. He talked to people about the ordinary things of their lives—the farmer plowing in the field, the woman cooking in the kitchen, clothes that were patched, and the building of houses. He understood the day-by-day problems and cares of human life.

Jesus sought to be the friend of all who would claim him. There was Matthew, a greedy tax-collector; James and John, simple fishermen; Mary and Martha, housekeepers; and the woman at the well who really was of the street. An interesting experience is to go through the record and list the friends of Jesus and study how he dealt with them. I do not recall one instance where he spoke harshly to a sinner; but as they associated with him, they became different.

Those who read the gospel record know that Jesus was not a weak, unreal person. There was a tenderness about him, yet there was also steel in him. He laughed but he also was stern. He loved but he never compromised. As ordinary people came to know him, they began to think about living in extraordinary ways. Friends of Jesus became ashamed of their sin. Some refused his friendship, and others were unwilling to make the changes which friendship with him demanded. Thank God, a few stayed close to him and gradually began to think as he thought. They never became perfect as he was perfect, but they did set him as their goal and they did head in his direction.

The New Testament tells us that after he died, he rose again and that he continues to live, and that he is even among us this very day. Jesus Christ is alive! When that great truth takes possession of a person, the process of salvation has truly begun. The fact of the living Christ means that people here and now can enter into transforming friendship with him. One may turn his back upon Christ and refuse his presence, but when one becomes his friend, then one who was lost has been found.

As a young man in high school it used to worry me when someone asked, "Are you saved?" I really did not know what was meant. If to be saved meant I had to be free of all sin and perfect in my life, then I fell far short of the mark. If to be a Christian meant that I must be like Christ, then I could not at all claim to be one. I went through some very discouraging times until I came upon the Lord's words, "I am the way" (John 14:6). That was something I could understand and accept.

"I am the way." Here is a highway stretching to another city. If I get on that road and start in that direction, then I am surely on the way. That does not mean I have arrived. I may be only a mile or so along the way while others may be ten miles, thirty miles, even a hundred miles ahead of me. But if one has found the way, he is not lost. As I see it, that is the Christian life.

Conversion means that I am committed to the way, and I begin a journey which is to continue the remainder of my days. As I travel, I come nearer and nearer to thinking as he thinks and living as he lives. Sometimes I become discouraged when I think of how far I yet have to go, but I take heart when I look back and realize I have made some progress. Beyond conversion, the Christian life is a journey in which our understanding is constantly enlarged and our commitment is made more complete.

Recently I was speaking on the matter of human relations. During a question-and-answer period, one member of the audience produced a newspaper column which I wrote fifteen years ago and quoted some statements I had made. I happily replied that I do not now stand where I was when I wrote that column. During these years I have made some progress. When I wrote the words which were held before me, my attitude was merely one of tolerance, but I have moved a real distance toward brotherhood. I was on the way fifteen years ago, but I am farther along the way now—and I hope to be still farther tomorrow.

Jesus said, "Ye must be born again" (John 3:7). Evangelism's effort is to bring about the new birth, but evangelism is concerned with a continuing effort. I am now a proud grandfather. Someone said, "Have I told you about my grandchild?" His friend replied, "No, and I surely do appreciate it." I could write many pages telling about the development of that precious baby, but the point is that day by day he is learning and becoming stronger, and I hope one day he will develop into real manhood.

There are many methods of evangelism. Preaching is one method. The goal of evangelism is to bring a person into relationship with Jesus Christ as Savior, Lord, and Friend. First as Savior, which is the result of the new birth. Then as Lord, in which he is supreme in every area of our lives. This requires enlightenment and new understandings. Finally as Friend, where one feels at home with him and in his way.

In the pages of this book are sermons by many men. Each is an evangelistic sermon, which means that each is a call to commitment to Christ. The sermons vary in tone and language. None of us is like any other man. But we who have been called by our Lord to care for his sheep—and more especially to rescue those sheep not in the fold—have a common denominator in all of our proclaiming of the Word of eternal life. That central emphasis—our passion, our *raison d'être*—is that "we've a story to tell to the nations"—beginning with individual men and women who await our word that they may be filled "with all joy and peace in believing" (Rom. 15:13).

Our lives as preachers are encumbered with many chores and responsibilities, some vital and some we feel trivial in terms of the main thrust of our calling. Our main labor must never be permitted to be obscured and lost. This is to bring hungering, sin-sick human brethren to the foot of the Cross of him who is the way—and then to help them to grow strong in the faith and grace of our Lord and Savior. To this end we were called, and for this purpose the Lord sustains and encourages us.

# I
# THE ALL-SUFFICIENT
# SAVIOR

# 1. The Focus of Faith

MERRILL C. TENNEY

•

The gospel of God . . . concerning his Son Jesus Christ our Lord.
ROMANS 1:1, 3

Like a trumpet call penetrating the din and confusion of a battlefield, these opening words of Paul's Epistle to the Romans declare the central truth of the Christian faith that Jesus Christ is the Son of God and the Lord of men. They affirm the central creed from which Christian ethic and devotion flow, that the eternal God has once for all revealed himself to the world through a Person whose historical reality affords the empirical foundation for assured belief. His character and utterances afford a key to the comprehension of God's nature and attitude toward humanity and his personal claims establish the relationship that man must maintain with God.

I. The gospel of God implies an initial factual basis, for a faith founded on abstractions or legend is only speculation or superstition. Irrespective of the varying interpretations given to the person of Jesus, whether hostile or favorable, sane and honest scholars will at least admit his historical existence. The main facts of his life and death, and the rise of the community that bears his name, are recorded in the secular historians of antiquity as well as in the New Testament which the Church produced. The assertion of the Soviets that Jesus never existed except as a capitalistic myth is unsupported by existing evidence. He cannot be the product of theological imagination, for he could be invented only by his equal. Among all the great figures of the past, he is unique because of the perfection of his character and the wide extent of his influence.

II. The effect of his life upon his closest associates has been recorded in the Gospels. According to their testimony, his teaching excelled that of all other religious leaders in its originality, simplicity, and depth. He devoted his brief ministry to the common people, feeding the hungry, teaching the ignorant, and healing the sick. The ultimate tragedy of his career epitomized his exceptional attitude, for he died with an audible prayer of forgiveness for his executioners. Three days after burial, his tomb was mysteriously vacant, and Mark's brief, unsophisticated account implies that neither Jesus' friends nor foes could supply any acceptable natural solution for the phenomenon. The extraordinary nature of this Person evokes wonder and leads to faith.

III. Insofar as his life is different from that of others, it must have a greater significance. His enemies recognized that he possessed unusual authority, for they said of him, "Never man spake like this man" (John 7:46). His disciples, who had observed more of his activity than others, and who had heard more of his teaching, solemnly concurred with Peter's confession, "We believe and are sure that thou art that Christ, the Son of the living God" (John 6:69). They interpreted his death by affirming that he "bare our sins in his own body on the tree, that we, being dead to sins, should live unto righteousness" (1 Pet. 2:24). They explained the empty tomb by saying that "it was not possible that he should be holden of [death]" (Acts 2:24). In him they found the living revelation of God.

If Jesus was an historical character, and if he was what he and his disciples claimed him to be, he has an inescapable relevance for our personal lives. In him God has entered the arena of human life, not as a visiting spectator, but as a participant in the totality of human misery and need. He came to exemplify God's holiness, to explain God's purpose for the world, and to accomplish human redemption. By assuming the burden of our sins he has discharged the debt that we could not pay, and by his resurrection he has demonstrated the triumph of God over evil and death. He is therefore a living person whom we must regard as a real though invisible contemporary, and whom we must either reject or accept by a final act of commitment to his sovereignty and salvation.

## 2. Which Savior?

JAMES FORRESTER

•

> Art thou he that should come, or do we look for another? MATTHEW
> 11:3

The picture of John the Baptist has been etched in a few strong lines in Biblical history. He was the last prophet of the Hebrew economy. He was a man of the open spaces who spoke the vernacular of the countryside. His manner was stern and impatient, and he lacked any sense of cautious diplomacy.

He preached an imminent judgment. Perhaps he thought that God would bare the sword of his righteous wrath and smite the people with some cataclysmic upheaval. He looked for one "whose fan is in his hand, and he will throughly purge his [threshing] floor, and will gather the wheat into his garner; but the chaff he will burn with fire unquenchable" (Luke 3:17).

Yet it was John who pointed with identifying finger to Christ and said, "Behold the Lamb of God, which taketh away the sin of the world" (John 1:29). It was he who baptized him in Jordan and smote the conscience and consciousness of men with the news of God's mighty outreach for the human heart through Jesus Christ.

I. The scene is changed in the eleventh chapter of Matthew.

John is languishing in prison. His friends bring reports to him and he listens in vain for the lightning bolts of judgment falling upon the people. Wickedness continues unabated and unpunished from the court to the market place. And what of Christ? He is "meek and lowly in spirit" and "goes about doing good."

In his deep perplexity John sent two of his friends to ask Christ directly, "Art thou he that should come, or do we look for another?" This was the crucial question for John the Baptist, but it is also the ultimate question for every twentieth-century person. Confronted with the human dilemma, every man must face the inescapable fact that Christ has come. He stands in the midst of the centuries as the living Word of God. He invites men to reconciliation with God by the Cross. He invites men to "newness of life" by the open tomb.

II. The religious attempts of man to diagnose his real problem and find an adequate answer to his dilemma burden the pages of philosophy and religion in a million books. They are marked by the shrines and temples, the rituals and symbols of the religions of the Orient and of the Occident.

The nonreligious attempts of our day take the form of "scientism." This is a creed which believes in the ultimate competence of the human mind to answer all the questions man can ask. In America we have assumed that the accumulation of vast amounts of scientific information about the physical universe will resolve the issues of life. The assumption is that our basic problem is an ignorance of physical laws and hence, the answer is free and universal secular education. But attitudes are more crucial than facts. We are "ever learning and never coming to the knowledge of the truth." It is paradoxical that our godless brilliance provides no guarantee that our passions will not override our intellectual judgments. The destruction of sixty-three million persons in scientific wars in the first half of our century may be only the prologue to the tragedy of a nuclear holocaust.

Modern man does not ask the right questions because he

wishes to avoid the spiritual realities. He loses the sense of God and of tomorrow in his obsession with his affluent but uneasy present.

The Bible makes central to the human problem the broken relationships of man with God, with himself, and with his fellow men. "All we like sheep have gone astray; we have turned every one to his own way" (Isa. 53:6). The Bible is also radical in its answer that God's way is not a list of human resolves or pious amendments but a "new creature." The Cross of Christ, the symbol of his reconciling and forgiving grace, is central in God's plan. Unique among all the religions of the world is our belief that God gave himself to save us and that suffering is redemptive.

III. Do we look for another? There is no other. There need be no other. There can be no other. Others have come. None was human enough and none was "God blessed forever." Others left writing, rituals, and followers when they died. Our Lord left his life, the presence of the Holy Spirit, the possibility of a new life, and an undying hope for every man. The lists are closed. None less than God can save, and God in Christ is reconciling us unto himself. We may discover him now. Because God himself has spoken in Christ, he is rightly imperious and sufficient. He is the irreducible minimum. "Without me ye can do nothing" (John 15:5). He is the immeasurable maximum. "In him dwelleth all the fulness of the Godhead bodily. And ye are complete in him" (Col. 2:9-10).

Let us give him the loving yes of our hearts "for there is none other name under heaven given among men whereby we must be saved" (Acts 4:12).

> Thou, O Christ, art all I want;
> More than all in thee I find.

# 3. Our All-Sufficient Savior

W. A. CRISWELL

•

Let us therefore come boldly unto the throne of grace, that we may obtain mercy, and find grace to help in time of need. HEBREWS 4:16

Where is the border of Christ's garment today? Is there no hem for us to touch? Are we the poorer because Christ has gone back to the Father? No, our living Lord still walks in our midst today. Up to the mighty heart of God, to the very throne of grace, go the sorrows, tears, and sighs of our lives. We in our times may also come with our ailing bodies, fevered minds, sin-sick souls, and in faith touch the border of his garment and be made whole again.

Down through the ages he has been doing in his risen life the same wonders of grace and power that he did when he walked in Judæa and Galilee centuries ago. Since then, how many millions of crushed hearts have heard him say just what he said of old: "Come unto me, all ye that labour and are heavy laden, and I will give you rest" (Matt. 11:28); how many a sinful soul has heard him say, "Be thou clean" (Mark 1:41); how many a penitent has heard him say as distinctly as he said to the dying thief, "To-day shalt thou be with me in paradise" (Luke 23:43). To how many a bereaved soul has he repeated the consolation, "I am the resurrection, and the life: he that believeth in me, though he were dead, yet shall he live" (John 11:25). At how many an Emmaus has he made himself known in the breaking of bread! How often has he said to trembling and dispirited disciples just what he said in the upper room, "Let not your heart be troubled, neither let it be afraid" (John 14:27). Through the years his voice has been heard speaking peace and comfort and hope, and his presence has been bestowing it.

The throne of majesty and righteousness is unto us a throne of grace. *Come boldly.* Come as you are, say what you feel, ask what you need. Pour out your heart before him. Confess your sins, your fears, your wandering thoughts. How fully, openly, may we speak to God in the name of him who went through all our sorrows and trials and heartaches. For this purpose he was tempted, that he might be able to succor them that are tempted. He is filled with tender compassion. This belongs to the perfection of his priesthood. He knows from his experience on earth how poor, weak, sinful his disciples are. He is prepared to receive the wounded, sin-stained believer, to dry the tears of Simon Peter, to say to Paul, oppressed by the thorn in the flesh, "My grace is sufficient for thee" (2 Cor. 12:9). *Come boldly.* Draw near in full assurance. We trust and are safe. The feet may tremble but the rock on which they are set standeth firm and immovable. All the help we need is treasured up for us in heavenly places. His intercession possesses omnipotence. The government is on his shoulder and the Father heareth him always.

*Come boldly.* Jesus belongs to the sinner. From his infancy in Bethlehem to the garden of Gethsemane, from the agony on the Cross to his ascension high above all heavens, he belongs to us. His obedient life, his prayers and tears, his sacrifice on the Cross, his glorious resurrection, his intercession in glory, all are ours. In the heavenly glory he is ours. In Jesus God is ours. In the ocean of his love, in the fullness of his grace, we can rejoice. Our very life is hid with Christ in God.

## 4. Do You Really Know Jesus?

JOHN R. BROKHOFF

•

As Jesus passed on from there, he saw a man called Matthew sitting at the tax office; and he said to him, "Follow me." And he arose and followed him. MATTHEW 9:9, RSV

A group of Manhattan ministers waited more than five hours to hear Dr. Leslie D. Weatherhead of London, whose ship was delayed because of fog. When at last Dr. Weatherhead went to the pulpit, he said, "Brethren, you have waited a long time and I have traveled a long distance to consider one simple question, 'Do you really know Jesus?'"

I. Is it not possible to know all about Jesus and at the same time not to know him personally? One well-known cleric claims that ninety per cent of his church members do not really know Jesus. God-fearing Job, at the end of his heart-rending experience, confessed, "I have heard of thee by the hearing of the ear: but now mine eye seeth thee" (Job 42:5).

John Wesley, an ordained clergyman of the Church of England, was so zealous in his calling that he went to America to convert the Indians. During a storm on the Atlantic, he was extremely frightened and asked a calm Moravian, "Are you not afraid?" He replied, "Why should I be afraid? I know Jesus Christ." Then looking into the eyes of Wesley, he asked, "Do you know Jesus Christ?" For the first time in his life, Wesley realized that he did not know Jesus personally. He had cherished the opportunity to convert the Indians, but who would convert him?

A man named Matthew was at work in his tax office when Jesus entered and sat opposite his desk. This was a personal confrontation: man to man, eye to eye, and heart to heart. Looking into the eyes of Matthew, Jesus said, "Follow me."

II. Really to know Jesus we too must have a face-to-face confrontation with him. How is this possible nearly two thousand years after Jesus left the earth? We should think it to be wonderful if Jesus were to come physically into our offices or into our kitchens and sit across the table from us. This indeed would be a genuine personal experience with Jesus. But this privilege is denied us.

Yet, Jesus does come to us today in and through his body, the Church. Christ confronts us in his Word which the Church preaches, teaches, and administers. When the Church calls us to serve, Christ is calling us. When the Gospel is preached, Christ is saying, "Follow me." Even at this late hour in history every man may have a personal experience with Jesus through the Word and the sacraments of the Church.

The possibility of really knowing Jesus rests upon the fact that Jesus is a living Presence in our midst. It has been said that the first Christians never really needed to remember Jesus, for Jesus was always with them. He was not dead, nor was he a past experience. Jesus was with them, and they introduced him to every man they met.

III. To know Jesus we must realize that he is more than a famous historical personality. For most people Jesus is almost exclusively associated with the past. He is, of course, like Socrates, Alexander the Great, Plato, Paul, Luther, and Washington, a towering figure in history. Accordingly, we are separated from him by twenty centuries, and we should expect his image to become dimmer with every passing year. When a high school student visited the Gettysburg battlefield and saw the cannon and breastworks, she exclaimed, "This is the first time I realized that the Civil War was more than just reading matter." Jesus, however, is more than a character out of a history book, for he lives today for all to know him.

To know Jesus we must also avoid the common practice of thinking of him only as a paragon of virtue. We put him on a high pedestal. He is the apex of all that is good and lovely. We admire and honor him. Having done all this, we then feel that as Christians we must emulate him, live like him, and walk in his steps. After a while, we abandon our efforts and turn away in frustration, because he is too high and holy for us. Our trouble is that we have thought of him as an impossible ideal.

Furthermore, to know Jesus we must not circumscribe him in the terminology of doctrines and creeds. Christianity is expressed and interpreted through such cardinal teachings as the Incarnation, the Atonement, the Ressurection, and the Parousia. But to have mastered these important concepts is not the same as knowing Jesus personally. Christians love and serve, not the creeds, but the Christ of the creeds.

IV. All true Christians have known Jesus face to face. Paul confronted Christ on the way to Damascus. Augustine learned to know Christ when he heard the words in a garden, "Take and read . . . take and read." St. Francis, meditating at a wayside shrine, heard Jesus say to him, "Go and sell all you have and give to the poor." While preparing his university lectures, Luther found Christ in the words, "The just shall live by faith" (Gal. 3:11). John Wesley learned to know Christ for the first time in a prayer meeting on Aldersgate Street. On page after page in Christian history we find similar experiences.

The average Christian, raised in a Christian home, has attended church and Sunday school habitually since childhood. But does he know Jesus personally, individually, actually? Is Jesus outside his life? Is he formal, objective, and somewhat theoretical? Has he never come inside the heart as a personal possession?

In many homes a picture of Christ has been hung on a wall. If Christ is really to be known, he must step out of that picture and into the heart of the viewer, for Christ is best known as a personal friend, a constant companion, and the living Lord of life whom we love and obey.

Luther said, "If you should knock on the door of my heart and ask, 'Who lives here?' I would not answer, 'Luther lives here; but Christ lives here.' " Christ is knocking on the door of your heart and asks, "Who lives here?" Take him into your heart that you too may reply, "Christ lives here."

## 5. Life's Most Important Question

CHARLES F. JACOBS

•

Who do men say that the Son of man is? MATTHEW 16:13, RSV

Jesus was in trouble. He had begun his ministry among his own people. Almost immediately he was involved in a series of conflicts with his Galilean foes. Those who opposed him increased in numbers and hatred, and he realized that violent death was a possibility. He wanted to be sure that if anything happened to him personally, his cause would live on to grow in the minds and the hearts of his followers. In this serious situation he asks his disciples, "Who do men say that the Son of man is?" They tell him what the crowds are saying. Then he personalizes the question: "But who do you say that I am?"

I. Many answers have been given, complementing or contradicting Peter's affirmation: "You are the Christ, the Son of the living God." Some have argued that Jesus was only a myth, a wishful fantasy. Others have said that he was a deluded visionary, an impractical dreamer. To countless millions he has been "the human face of God," "the fairest among ten thousand," and the hope of the world. These appraisals underline Emerson's saying that the name of Jesus "is not so much written as ploughed into the history of the world."

"Who do men say that the Son of man is?" remains the most important question on the agenda of our time. A world of consequences, for good or for ill, hangs upon our answer.

II. If others had their ideas about Jesus, he had some

thoughts of his own concerning his significance. He believed that he had a commission from God to establish the kingdom of God on earth. This kingdom had already come in part, for, as he said to those about him, "The kingdom of God is within you" (Luke 17:21). The duty of his followers is to bring it into fuller realization. He said, "I am the way." If men would forsake the old ways and walk with him, they would experience the reign of God in their own lives. "I am the door," he said, and through that doorway they could pass into the presence of the Eternal. The organizing principle of the universe is love. He called it God. The power of God working through human hearts can overcome the strangeness and the hatreds that divide men. He dramatized the power of love so effectively in his own life that men who had not known him in the flesh would repeat the words, "The Word was made flesh, and dwelt among us" (John 1:14).

III. Our Lord's greatness was the fruit of his own faith in God, his unwillingness to return hate for hate, his trust in his fellow men, and, above all, his refusal to be their master and his readiness to be their servant. It gives me pain to think that Jesus, so gentle and so wise, was nailed to the Cross; yet I am heartened when I remember that his accusers have gone down to ignominious graves, while he lives on in the souls of men as a mighty and inspiring influence.

Jesus said, "I am the way, the truth, and the life: no man cometh unto the Father, but by me" (John 14:6). That is the basic fact of our faith—and our eternal hope.

# 6. The Things Touching the King

HORATIUS BONAR

•

What think ye of Christ? MATTHEW 22:42

The Lord's question here was specially meant for Jews. They were expecting Messiah, *the* Christ, and studying Scripture to know what had been written of him; and so our Lord asks, What is your opinion of the Christ? Is it according to the Scriptures? Are you of one mind with Moses, with David, with the prophets, with God himself, concerning him?

This was Christ's question to the Jews; it is his question to us in these last days.

What are your views on the points connected with Jesus of Nazareth? Are they true or false? scriptural or unscriptural?

1. *As to his person.* Is he God to you? Is he man to you? Son of God and Son of man? Immanuel? The Word made flesh? God manifest in flesh?

2. *As to his work.* Is it to you the work of a sinbearer? Is it finished? And are you enjoying it as finished or only half finished? His blood, his righteousness, his cross, what are they to you?

3. *As to his kingdom.* Is it a righteous yet also a glorious kingdom to you? Do you understand the mode and the terms of entrance? the new birth, and simple faith in the King?

On these three great points are your views right or wrong? Are you of one mind with God as to each of them? To be of one mind with God is faith; not to be of one mind is unbelief. Naturally we are wrong on these points. The Scripture, through the teaching of the Holy Ghost, sets us right.

1. *Is thy understanding right as to these things?* Dost thou *know* them?

23

2. *Is thy heart right as to them?* Dost thou feel them? Hast thou not only got hold of them, but have they got hold of thee?

3. *Is thy life right as to them?* Art thou a better, truer, holier, and more earnest man because of them? Is thy whole life, thy whole being, outer and inner, molded by them? Or are there still other influences working more powerfully than these? If thy understanding and heart have received these, then thy *life* will show this. There will be fruit unto holiness. The truth, the joy, the light, will shine *through* thee, and shine out from thee, on all around.

What then think ye of Christ? Is he such as you can love and trust?

1. *As a Savior.* Is he the Savior that suits thee? And dost thou appreciate his great salvation? Are you glad to have him for your Savior? Or have you any fault to find with him as such? Would some change in his person or work have made him more suitable?

2. *As a friend.* Is he the friend you need? Is his the friendship, the *kind* of friendship, that suits your circumstances, your feelings, your temperament? Is his the kind of sympathy and counsel and wisdom which you feel you need from a friend?

3. *As an advocate.* You need intercession and one to plead for you. Does his advocacy suit you? Can you trust him with your case? Can you put everything in his hands, that he may manage all your concerns for you? Do you see how successful he has been with every case he has undertaken, not losing one, and can you trust him with yours—his skill, wisdom, love, argument, eloquence? Is Jesus Christ the righteous, just the kind of advocate you need? and are you just the client for such an advocate?

4. *As a King.* Is he just such a King as you should like—as suits you—as suits this earth—as suits the universe? And what say you to him as a Judge? You that shall never come into condemnation, do you enjoy the thought of him as the Judge? You that are still under condemnation, what think ye of him as a

Judge? What do you say to his being *your* Judge? What think ye of standing before him and giving in your account to him?

What think ye of Christ? Do you say, "I think him the chief among ten thousand"? It is well. Do you say, "I know not what to think"? Ah, take heed, there is something wrong within you, if not all wrong together. Do you give no answer? It matters not. We shall soon find it out. By the company you keep; the books you read; the way in which you lay out your talents and the time and money; the way you transact business; your dealings in the market; your conduct at home; your letters and correspondence; your conversation with neighbors— by these we shall find out what you think of him.

## 7. Our Interceding Savior

GEORGE H. MORRISON

●

> He is able also to save them to the uttermost . . . seeing he ever liveth to make intercession for them. HEBREWS 7:25

I. Our text tells us that somebody is praying for us, and the somebody is our risen Savior. That is the only meaning which our text can bear, and with all its mystery we thankfully accept it. Others may forget us in their prayers; there is One in heaven who never does forget. Others may fail us when their lamp burns low; *he* ever liveth. We are engirdled by the prayers of One who loves us and has the ear of God, and therefore is able to save unto the uttermost.

II. Nor was this ministry begun in heaven; it was carried over from the days on earth. Our Lord on earth was an interceding Savior. One remembers his words to Simon Peter, recorded in the Gospel of St. Luke: "Simon . . . Satan hath desired to have you . . . but I have prayed for thee, that thy faith fail not" (Luke 22:31-32). And if our Lord so prayed when he was here, why should it be thought a thing incredible that he continue that ministry in heaven? Did he not say, "I will pray the Father, and he shall give you another Comforter" (John 14:16)? Have we never experienced with an inward certainty that in the hour of need that Comforter has come? All fresh enduements of the Holy Spirit, whether for service or for suffering, are intimations of a praying Savior.

III. We remember another intercession, "Father, forgive them; for they know not what they do" (Luke 23:34). And if he prayed that prayer when on the Cross, we may be perfectly certain that forgiveness followed. So much of our sin is not deliberate. Evil is wrought by want of thought. We are such ignorant and foolish beings that we can rarely follow our actions to their issues. But he is praying for us just as he prayed on Calvary, and he is able to save unto the uttermost, because he ever liveth to make intercession for us.

IV. Prayer is never an isolated thing. Whenever anybody prays for you, it means that he bears you on his heart. If our Lord is praying for us in his ascension, that tells us he has not forgotten us, but is eager to help us in our need. Prayers are mockeries that do not lead to action. True prayer issues in endeavor. Unless we are willing to help the man we pray for, our prayers are nothing else than empty breath. Thus do we reach our assurance of his help, when the way is dark and the heart is very sore, from the good news with which the Gospel rings, that he ever liveth to make intercession for us.

# 8. No Alternative!

GILBERT L. GUFFIN

•

He that is not with me is against me; and he that gathereth not with me scattereth abroad. MATTHEW 12:30
Lord, to whom shall we go? thou hast the words of eternal life. JOHN 6:68

One of the most wonderful as well as the most frightening facts in life is that we have choices to make. We are free to make our choices, but the alternative to the right choice may be disaster.

We may choose to be with Christ or against him. "He that is not with me," says Christ, "is against me." But if we choose to be against him, keep in mind that he who "gathereth not with [him] scattereth." We have a choice, you see, but is the alternative tolerable? We may go with Christ or away from him, but what are the consequences if we go away?

In facing our decision there are three facts we ought to ponder.

I. *A substitute for Christ is unavailable.* "To whom shall we go?" asked the early disciples in solemn dismay at the thought. The question is as timely as when first asked. Indeed, to whom shall we go? To whom may we go?

Everything man has tried has failed—except Christ. Everything else to which he has turned has been as the worship of a compass that told us nothing while we drifted on a vessel we knew not how to guide on seas too much for us.

Let us write the fact indelibly upon the imperishable tablet of our memories that for the salvation of us men and our world a substitute for Christ is unavailable. If Christ cannot save us, then our case is hopeless.

II. *An alternative for Christ is unneedful.* If in a world where there is no evidence of hope for our salvation in anything on the horizon of knowledge besides Christ, and Christ himself should seem inadequate, then what Stygian darkness would lie across our future. But, thank heaven, no such appalling possibility confronts us. When one really meets Christ, he becomes as certain as his disciples of old and will say with them, "Thou hast the words of eternal life"!

The evidence of this? "Judge" Christ on the basis of his words. "Judge" Christ on the basis of his works. "Judge" Christ on the basis of his sheer personal worthiness. Judged by his words, by his works, and above all by his worthiness, no substitute is needed for Christ in our world. What is needed is a serious purpose to do his will, a solemn intent to carry out his plans, and a steadfast effort to grow like him in thought and act.

III. *An alternative to Christ is unbearable.* "He that is not with me is against me," Christ keeps saying, "and he that gathereth not with me scattereth." "Scattereth"—what a significant word! Those who come not with him have no place to go. They must wander forever. Always going somewhere, but never arriving; always seeking, but never finding; always flying away from center, never finding it. These are the real eccentrics, those who are away from center. These are the problems of our world. They scatter and cause others to scatter.

In a day when the world is critically imperiled not simply by what is in the hydrogen bomb but also by what is in the heart of man, and when it is growing more obvious that in Christ is our only hope for the solution of the major needs of mankind and for man's salvation eternally, is not to decline his call to be "with" him really to be "against" him? Is not the failure to follow him not only to decline to have a part in the solution of human need but, even worse, to be a part of the problem of our world? This is to be against him. This is neutrality that involves complicity, and such complicity is sin.

The Christ for whom no substitute is available and no alternative is needful becomes the Christ for whom no other choice is bearable.

## 9. The Cross as Love's Necessity

W. M. CLOW

•

He saved others; himself he cannot save. MATTHEW 27:42

It was not the Roman guard who compelled him to his Cross, and not the driven nails which held him to its beams. "No man taketh [my life] from me, but I lay it down of myself (John 10:18). "The cup which my Father hath given me, shall I not drink it" (John 18:11). "Thus it behoved Christ to suffer" (Luke 24:46). We see him dying for the noblest purpose the human mind can conceive. There is really no other purpose great but the redeeming of man, body, soul, and spirit, from the dominion of evil, and the restoring of the image of God upon him. Every pure purpose among men is but its faint reflection; every holy vocation only the fulfilling of its service. And we see him dying in an almost incredible and quite inexhaustible love—a love which no wrong could change and no sorrow could quench.

The necessity of his sacrifice of himself for our salvation touches those infinite mysteries which seem to grow darker the more eagerly we look into them. Because they are infinite, because our knowledge of such "heavenly things" must be imperfect and provisional, and because our understanding of spiritual verities is greatly dependent on our personal experience, we should be gentle in our confidence and patient with each other. We can be sure that the same inexorable necessity for sacrifice which ordains that the well-being of men shall come only through the costly sacrifice of its best and noblest, prevails in the highest sphere of all. If God and man are to be reconciled, if the sense of guilt is to be taken from human consciences, if the love of God is to be manifested to man, if man is to see and know that God's love for man and his longing for his holiness are the constant passion of God's heart, if a new conception of holiness, and of service, and of love is to dawn upon men's minds, a new desire to seek after its attainment to be born in their hearts, and a new power to press forward to it to be infused into their wills, the sacrifice of the Cross seems to any man to whom God and his law are realities, the supreme necessity. With any man for whom God and our accountability to him are meaningless terms, we have no question to consider. This is certain, as not only the New Testament saints, but millions now living do testify, that the sacrifice of Jesus on his Cross has done these very things; that for them the necessity has been felt in the hours of their holiest experiences, and the issue of it is, that they have been saved—saved from a dark fear of God, from the awful judgment on their sin, from the power of it and the love of it. That consequent which, by universal testimony, has only one cause, affirms that cause to be its necessity. "He saved others; himself he cannot save" becomes an anthem for redeemed and adoring men.

This high truth may remain for many greatly dark. Humble souls are saved, put their trust in the mercy of God in Christ, and follow peace and holiness, who could not say one word for the sweet reasonableness and alluring grace of the profound doctrine which holds the truth in its keeping. But for all, whether humbly content with the assurance of salvation, or eager to know the mysteries behind, there is an indispensable experience. That, and that alone, illumines. When a human soul passes through that spiritual travail known as conviction of sin (and that may be in his early years, or it may visit him long after manhood has come to him, and very solemn vows have been taken), when God and conscience become the great certainties, when some deed of iniquity stands out in condemning and inexcusable blackness, or his very nature shocks him by its corruption, when shame haunts him by day and unrest vexes him by night, then he will look at the Cross, then he will accept the mercy of God, and then he will understand the necessity of sacrifice in salvation—but not till then. "It is the heart that makes the theologian"; for the simple reason that only the heart, that is, the inner core of a man's being—his desires, aims, impulses, will—is quickened by conviction of sin. For a man who has not felt the shame and the burden of sin, and realized it to be the barrier that keeps him back from God, to see love's necessity in the Cross is as vain as for a childless man to interpret the thoughts of a father, or a deaf man to expound a theory of music. "The natural man receiveth not the things of the Spirit of God" (1 Cor. 2:14).

## 10. The Hunger for a Right Guy
### CHARLES LYON SEASHOLES

•

And there were also two . . . malefactors. . . . We receive the due reward of our deeds: but this man hath done nothing amiss. LUKE 23:32, 41

The flag at Leavenworth Penitentiary was at half-mast on Lincoln's Birthday. Punch Pinero, alien from Italy, was mystified. The other men whose stories are related in *My Six Convicts* finally told him who Abraham Lincoln was. Punch then said, "Was he a right guy?" "Doc," the psychologist and author of the book, assured him he was. The convicts began to hum and then sing "The Battle Hymn of the Republic." The psychologist, Donald Powell Wilson, writes, "My spine began to tingle. . . . I was thinking now of the old hunger in men for a right guy and their veneration for him when they find him."

This hunger for a right guy reveals a wonderful thing about human nature, that men can picture to themselves a right guy, even when, by and large, and some would say, basically, they are not themselves right guys.

This hunger for a right guy is not just to see one but also to be one. Human nature has something in it that prompts men to want to be more than they are or better than they are. Christianity appeals to men because it meets this hunger in him whose name we Christians bear.

Max Schoen, author of *The Man Jesus Was* and a Jew, said, "There had to be a Jesus." The religious development of the Hebrew people had reached the place where there had to be a Jesus who in his own life incarnated the best of that heritage.

We are never so certain that we are not right guys as when we look at Jesus. But we are never so certain that we want to be right guys as when he looks at us with the appeal and challenge with which he looked at his disciples. Peter felt his unworthiness. "Depart from me; for I am a sinful man, O Lord" (Luke 5:8). But the One before whom he felt his unworthiness was one who saw the potential in Peter and "called the unknown best from Peter, James, and all the rest."

The deepest hunger in men is for the kind of God of whom the Old Testament speaks: "Shall not the Judge of all the earth do right?" (Gen. 18:25). G. A. Studdert-Kennedy's poem "Well?" records the dream of a cockney soldier, who, in a place beyond this world, is confronted by Someone.

> "What was 'E like?" you're askin' now.
>   Can't word it anyway,
> 'E just were 'Im, that's all I knows.

The One he saw was him in whose eyes were all the eyes of those who had wronged this soldier and those whom he had wronged.

> And then at last 'E said one word,
>   'E just said one word—"Well?"
> And I said in a funny voice,
>   "Please can I go to 'Ell?"
>
>               *
>
> And then 'E answered "No,
> You can't that 'Ell is for the blind,

> And not for those that see.
> You know that you 'ave earned it, lad,
>     So you must follow Me.
> Follow Me on by the paths o' pain,
>     Seeking what you 'ave seen,
> Until at last you can build the 'Is'
>     Wi' the brick o' the 'Might 'ave been.' "

It is never too early to begin to be a right guy and to settle the aims, ideals, principles, and even more, the preferences of your life. Often this comes down to what Rufus Jones gave as the words of a woman who was at Hull House: "I'd druther."

It is never too late to begin again to be a right guy. Jesus might have written a book entitled *My Two Convicts*. Luke called them malefactors. One let a grudge against society blot out everything else, and he raged against Jesus. The other saw in Jesus "a right guy" and knew that he himself was not a right guy. So rebuking the other, he said, "This man has suffered unjustly, but we justly." Then he reached out for something. "Remember me." He got his assurance.

It is never too late to begin again to be a right guy. You ask, "How can I make it right?" That is not the first or primary concern. God can make you right. He is that kind of God, and then he and you together can begin to make your life right.

You may then do as Studdert-Kennedy said:

> "Until at last you can build the 'Is'
>     Wi' the brick o' the 'Might 'ave been.' "

Christ can make you right with him, right with yourself, and right with those for whose regard your heart hungers.

# II
# THE MEANING
# OF SALVATION

## 11. How to Be Saved

W. E. SANGSTER

●

By grace are ye saved through faith. EPHESIANS 2:8

I. What do we mean by grace? The old definition called it "the free, unmerited favor of God." On that definition I cannot improve. It means that at the heart of all true communion with God there lies this deep truth, that God himself took the initiative. He loves us better than we can ever love him. He loves us with a love that does not depend on any answering love of ours. We have not to earn his love, any more than we earned our mother's love. We have but to receive it.

Always the initiative is from God! When you first came to him, if indeed you have come to him, you came because he first drew you. The very faith by which you lay hold of him is not of yourself; this also is a gift of God. Nor is it only in the beginning that your salvation is God's free gift. Every onward step you have made in your spiritual pilgrimage has been possible by some bestowing of his grace. Even the life of holiness, to which all the time he is seeking to bring you—the Christlike quality that he wants to repeat in all of his children—even that you have not to achieve but to receive. It is a gift of God.

II. Whenever we use the word "saved" some people at once think of hell or heaven. Being saved means to them just that: escaping hell; achieving heaven. But that is a very limited way

37

to think of this term "saved." For instance, it puts the whole matter in the future. Now we are on earth, not in heaven, and we can be saved now. The Scripture says, "Whosoever believeth in him . . . [hath] eternal life" (John 3:15). He has it here and now!

Salvation is not from earth, but from sin. It is deliverance not merely from the penalty of sin but also from the fact of sin. Those who are theological-minded may be thinking that I am confusing salvation and sanctification. Still I say that the outworking of salvation gives us deliverance from the sins of the flesh, and likewise from the sins of the mind.

Think of the men who have been hopelessly imprisoned by thirst for strong drink, and yet have been delivered from that bondage. Think of the men who have been eaten up with lust; whose heads, in the words of Montaigne, have been "merry-go-rounds of lustful images." Think of people in the grip of greed, who become as metallic as the coins they seek. All of these are victims of present sins, and from these present sins there is for each of them a present salvation.

Not only from the sins of the flesh! There is likewise deliverance from the sins of the mind. From jealousy, and all the canker that it brings; from gossip, and all the evil that it entails; from pride, the most subtle of sins. From all these there is salvation, here and now.

III. There are many definitions of faith. No definition can be satisfactory if it confines faith merely to belief. That would make it merely the mental acknowledgment of some external fact, and would not include at its very heart the spirit of trust. This is the keyword of faith; it means to "trust." Faith is not merely an expression of belief. It is a venture of the whole personality in trusting One who is worthy.

Let me ask, Are you conscious of your own need? At the same time are you aware of your weakness; of the pressure of your sins; of the dark problems in your life, and of your inability alone to grapple with them? Do you feel that you need the help of someone else? It is to such felt needs that the Gospel speaks about your being saved.

If you have never yet ventured on Christ, I plead with you to do so now. If you have already received a timorous faith, I urge you to venture on him far more completely; to recognize that the real end of faith is to unite the person who believes with the Person on whom he believes; and that only as you are united with Christ through faith can you have the quality of life which is the sterling of eternity.

## 12. What Must I Do to Be Saved?

CLARENCE EDWARD MACARTNEY

•

And suddenly there was a great earthquake. . . . And the keeper of the prison . . . fell down before Paul and Silas . . . and said, Sirs, what must I do to be saved? Acts 16:26-30

That faith is the only way to be saved is clearly shown when we take the great passages of Scripture dealing with this subject, and where the word "believe" is used, and substitute for it its Greek equivalent "have faith." The verb "believe" always comes from the noun "faith." Take these passages as examples, where we substitute "have faith" for "believe": "God so loved the world, that he gave his only begotten Son, that whosoever *hath faith* in him should not perish, but have everlasting life" (John 3:16). "Verily, verily, I say unto you, He that *hath faith* on me hath everlasting life" (John 6:47). "Go ye into all the world, and preach the gospel to every creature. He that *hath faith* and is baptized shall be saved" (Mark 16:15-16). "What must I do to be saved? . . . *Have faith* on the Lord Jesus Christ, and thou shalt be saved" (Acts 16:30-31). The offer of salvation is free; the gate to heaven is as wide as the mercy of God. But this free salvation is not unconditional. It has one, only one, but nevertheless *one* condition—the sinner's faith in Christ.

Since we are saved by faith, we know that our own character and our own good works have nothing to do with it. If Paul had told this jailer he could be saved by his past record, it would have been a message of despair, for he had no good works to which he could point. In the second place, such a way of salvation by faith in Christ signally honors the Son of God. God chooses not only to save man, but to save him in a way which shall glorify his Son. In the third place, this way of salvation is for us a free way and an easy way. Christ did the hard part. His were the tears, the groans, the sighs, the agony, the Cross, and the awful darkness. It is because the way was so hard for Christ that it is so easy for you. Indeed, so easy that some miss it altogether.

What a Christ we have in whom to have faith! To whom shall we go but unto him? Do you believe? Then prove it, as this jailer did by his acts of mercy and kindness and the joy of his heart. If you have not believed, will you not now believe? Why wait for that, and for him who is waiting for you? Do not question the truth of it. Do not be kept by a lack of feeling, or the lack of a good record, or a lack of what you think is fit repentance. What Christ said, what Paul said to the jailer, was not to *feel* this way or that way, *do* this or that, lay claim to this or that good act in the past, but *believe*, have faith in the Lord Jesus Christ, and thou shalt be saved. We cannot measure all that "have faith" means. But neither can we measure all that "thou shalt be saved" means. Perhaps, indeed, the jailer by this time could tell you and me something about it. But all that it does mean, for that we shall have to wait until we stand by the jailer's side before the throne of the Lamb, and sing our praise unto him who came to seek and to save that which was lost.

# 13. The Christian Dynamic

FRANK E. GAEBELEIN

•

I am not ashamed of the gospel of Christ: for it is the power [literally, "the dynamic"] of God unto salvation to every one that believeth. ROMANS 1:16

Our subject brings us to the center of Christianity, and confronts us with the power that makes it go. What is the power that the Apostle proclaims as the dynamic of God unto salvation? About this dynamic of God no one needs to be in any doubt. The Bible makes perfectly plain that the dynamic of God is the Gospel. We stand, therefore, on ground that is familiar to many of us. And yet is it not strange that people these days are willing to try every solution for the problems of life except plain, downright Christianity? What then is the Gospel?

I. *The Gospel centers in Christ*, the most important Person who has ever lived, not only because of what he did nineteen hundred years ago, but because of what he is doing now, with his life-changing, transforming power. Today he still has power to transform; whether in the slums of our cities or among respectable, educated sinners, he is changing the weak and the erring into strong children of God to whom he gives life more abundant.

II. *The Gospel centers in the Cross and in the Resurrection.* There alone is rock-bottom Christian truth. No one who has experienced the joy of release from the bondage of sin and guilt can ever think of these events as other than all-powerful, life-changing facts. Thousands of men have died as martyrs; only Christ has ever claimed to die for the sins of others, and today he is not dead. He alone has brought life and immortality to light through the Gospel.

"And now," writes Arnold Toynbee, "as we stand and gaze

with our eyes fixed upon the farther shore, a single Figure fills the whole horizon. There is the Savior. 'The pleasure of the Lord shall prosper in his hand; he shall see of the travail of his soul, and shall be satisfied.' " At the center of the New Testament, as at the center of the whole Bible, and of the entire Christian faith, is this fact of the crucified and risen, living and transforming, Christ.

III. Now I close with a simple invitation to acceptance of this Savior. After all, Christian preaching is proclaiming the Gospel for a personal decision. Believe me, Christ is still effective to meet the deepest needs of human life. But there is a condition. The dynamic of God operates through only one channel. In the words of our text, the Gospel is "the power of God unto salvation to every one that believeth." The only channel is belief, trust, personal commitment, to Jesus Christ.

John G. Paton, pioneer missionary to the New Hebrides in the Pacific, was hard put to find a word for "believe," in the sense of trust, in the language of the South Sea Islanders, for whom he was translating the New Testament. Finally he found the solution, by thus translating the answer of Paul and Silas to the question of the Philippian jailer, "What must I do to be saved?": "Lean your whole weight upon the Lord Jesus Christ and be saved." That is all, but that is enough, and vastly more.

## 14. The Kingly Purchase

### Louis H. Evans

•

For thou wast slain, and hast redeemed [purchased] us to God by thy blood out of every kindred, and tongue, and people, and nation; and hast made us unto our God kings and priests: and we shall reign on the earth. REVELATION 5:9-10

To whom do you and I belong? Deep in everyone's heart someone, something, wears a "crown." In a study of history it would be of more than passing interest to make a study of how kings came to own their subjects or to rule over them. We would find that some conquered the people by force, others by propaganda and enslavement of the people's minds, still others by intrigue. Christ came to his mastery by a loving purchase and, at least, this will be a part of the picture.

One of the reasons for this kingly ransom is found in our text. Before we mention this claim of God upon us, we might mention the other rights by which our personalities should belong to him. We are his, of course, by right of *creation*. The words "In the beginning God . . ." are an explanation of your life and mine. We are his by right of his sovereign creatorship. Again, we are his because of his daily *sustaining*. He is the Lord of life, and life is his gift. Our days are allotted to us by him who is our daily Sustainer. Finally, we are his by the right of his loving purchase.

How did we come upon this regal standing which we have with God? How did we become a part of this kingdom? The Greek word for "purchase" is *agoradzo*. The true meaning of this word will bring us to the Grecian, Roman, or Oriental market place as it functioned in the time of Christ. Here on the selling block stood men who were sold for debts they were unable to pay; because they were hopelessly in debt their freedom had been forfeited. The highest bidder purchased such a person as a *doulos* or slave, to be his own altogether and to serve him forever.

This was your condition and mine spiritually; we were "sold under sin" (Rom. 7:14). Spiritual debts had mortgaged our souls beyond any possibility of our paying or making remission for them. We had lost our spiritual right to freedom. Justice would decide that and preside over the merits or demerits of our lives. Suddenly God's Son offers himself: "I give my life a ransom." The Kingly One, by every right of this purchase, may step forward and claim us for his own. From that moment on, if we accepted the purchase, we became his—every atom of our being, every fiber of our mind and muscle, every ability of our lives. We became his "redeemed ones," his *douloi*, slaves of God, the servants of Christ!

Paul reminds us of this when he says, "Ye are not your own. For ye are bought with a price: therefore glorify God" (1 Cor. 6:19-20). Thus Christ "redeemed us" to God, out of every kindred blood and people and nation.

## 15. We Must Be Saved

THEODORE F. ADAMS

•

Neither is there salvation in any other: for there is none other name under heaven given among men, whereby we must be saved. ACTS 4:12

We use the word "saved" in a number of different ways. For example, a tunnel collapses and rescuers dig desperately to "save" the men who are trapped. A ship is in distress at sea and other ships hasten to "save" those who might otherwise be lost. We read of men injured in an isolated spot and a helicopter flies in to "save" them. Or we "save" money, meaning either we keep it or put it to good use.

Just what do we mean when we speak as Christians of individuals being "saved"? Why do we call Jesus "Savior"? We find one answer in the word about Jesus' coming: "Thou shalt call his name Jesus: for he shall save his people from their sins" (Matt. 1:21). He came to help us in our need, to save and keep us, and to put us to work in his kingdom.

"All have sinned, and come short of the glory of God" (Rom. 3:23). Each of us knows the feeling of guilt, the sense of failing others or ourselves, and the feeling of having missed the mark or fallen short of the best we know. We have sinned against God and others and against our own best selves. In desperation we seek some answer to our sin, some way out, someone who can "save" us from our sense of guilt.

I. To all who believe in Christ there comes the assurance found in the words of Peter about Jesus: "Neither is there salvation in any other: for there is none other name under heaven given among men, whereby we must be saved."

Peter spoke these words just after he and John had healed a crippled man at the gate of the Temple. As a crowd gathered, Peter said, "Repent, be converted, that your sins may be blotted out." When challenged to tell in whose name he had done this, he replied, "By the name of Jesus Christ of Nazareth, whom ye crucified, whom God raised again from the dead."

Our need for salvation is stressed in Peter's statement, "We must be saved." Measured by the standards of Christ, we all have sinned. We are guilty of sins of commission and omission. That is, we have done things we ought not to have done, and we have failed to do the best that we knew. We are guilty of sins of the flesh and such sins of the spirit as hatred, pride, envy, jealousy, malice, and selfishness.

II. We cannot save ourselves. We are too weak and sinful. We need a "power beyond ourselves that works for righteousness." Paul sensed this when he cried, "Wretched man that I am! who shall deliver me?" (Rom. 7:24). Jesus taught this to Nicodemus when he talked about the importance of spiritual as well as physical birth, saying, "Ye must be born again." We may well say with Nicodemus, "How can these things be?" (John 3:7, 9.) In God's plan of salvation he has his part and we have ours. "For God so loved the world, that he gave his only begotten Son, that whosoever believeth in him should not perish, but have everlasting life" (John 3:16). God sent his Son to save us. It is our responsibility to choose to believe in him and accept him as our personal Savior.

Jesus said, "The Son of man is come to seek and to save that which was lost" (Luke 19:10). He illustrated this in Luke 15 in the three stories about the lost coin, the lost sheep, and the lost boy. The coin and the sheep could not save themselves. The woman had to seek and find her lost coin. The shepherd had to seek and save the lost sheep. The boy, however, was different. The father was ready and eager to welcome the son back, to forgive and to forget, and to help him start anew; but the son had to make a decision for himself. When he came to himself, he said, "I will arise and go to my father" (Luke 15:18). And there was joy in that home, as there is joy in heaven, when a sinner repents and returns to the Father.

Sin is anything that separates us from God. It may be rebellion against his will, or the deliberate choice of evil, or carelessness or indifference, or loving things more than we love God. However, we have the promise: "If we confess our sins, he is faithful and just to forgive us our sins, and to cleanse us from all unrighteousness" (1 John 1:9). The way is made plain in the words, "With the heart man believeth unto righteousness; and with the mouth confession is made unto salvation" (Rom. 10:10). All of this is available to us by the forgiving grace of God. Grace means simply that God treats us, not as we deserve, but as we need. "By grace are ye saved through faith; and that not of yourselves: it is the gift of God" (Eph: 2:8).

It was this realization that came to John Newton. He lived a sordid and evil life for many years, but one day in a terrific storm at sea he called out to God for forgiveness. When he finally reached his home in England, he was a changed man and eventually became a minister. His amazement and joy in the forgiving and redeeming love of God was so real that he wrote the now familiar words:

> Amazing grace! how sweet the sound,
> That saved a wretch like me!
> I once was lost, but now am found,
> Was blind, but now I see.

He had to do his part to receive the forgiveness of God, and only as he did was he saved. So we too have our part to play in salvation.

III. I often tell our children that coming to Christ is as simple as ABC:

> A—Admit that you have sinned.
> B—"Believe on the Lord Jesus Christ, and thou shalt be saved" (Acts 16:31).
> C—Confess your sins and claim the forgiveness God has promised.

Or I express salvation in this manner:

> A—Accept Jesus Christ as your personal Savior and Lord.
> B—Be baptized on confession of your faith.
> C—Church membership naturally follows, for you take your place in the fellowship of baptized believers for Christian nurture and service.

But the ABC formula is incomplete until we add one more letter:

> D—Do whatever Christ commands.

When we call Jesus our Savior we speak chiefly of what he does for us. When we acknowledge him as Lord, we speak of what we must do for him. He has commanded us to be baptized and to seek to win others. We become workers with him as we go into all the world to preach the Gospel. We are saved to serve. Like the disciples, "We cannot but speak the things which we have seen and heard" (Acts 4:20).

Yes, we must be saved. We cannot save ourselves. Thank God there is one who can save us now and forever. Will you "believe on the Lord Jesus Christ and be saved"?

# 16. How We Come to See God

CHARLES A. TRENTHAM

•

Scripture: PROVERBS 3:5-8

At eventide a little boy came upon an old fisherman who was sitting on the riverbank. He said, "Mister, can anyone see God?" The old man looked down the river toward the beautiful and glorious setting sun and said, "Sonny, it's getting so I can't see anything but God."

Our generation is one in which bold and blatant atheism, cold and clamant agnosticism, militant and metallic materialism, arrogant and self-sufficient humanism, have woven a dark veil between the hearts of men and the face of God. We have forgotten George Santayana's words:

> It is not wisdom to be only wise,
> And on the inward vision close the eyes.

Why should we think it strange that we have no demonstrable proof of God's existence when John the Evangelist emphatically said, "No man hath seen God at any time" (John 1:18)? God is not an object to be seen. He is a person who discloses himself to us in interpersonal relationships. You do not come to know a person by looking at him nor by reasoning about him. You do not know a person by analyzing him.

A great philosopher once said, "A man may know all about the laws of light and yet, just because he knows those laws, he may miss the radiance of the sunset and the glory of the morning sky."

The wise man of old counsels us, "Be not wise in thine own eyes" (Prov. 3:7). The wisest of men have never discovered God without coming to the realization that it was not their discovery but God's disclosure which made the vision of God possible.

48

Those who think of 'God as man's discovery think more of the cleverness of man than of the grace of God. Every wise man of earth has been in quest of God. When they have found him, he has been disclosed in the person of Jesus Christ running with open arms down the road to meet them.

To see God the writer of Proverbs points us to three prerequisites:

I. "Trust in the Lord with all thine heart" (Prov. 3:5). Either we begin with God and see him through the eyes of faith or we never get to anything more than the creature of our own intellect.

Commitment to Christ is the first step toward seeing and understanding God. "But as many as received him, to them gave he power to become the sons of God, even to them that believe on his name" (John 1:12). Receiving Christ is prerequisite to the opening of our blind eyes and to even the belief which he fashions by his grace.

II. We also see God through eyes that are full of reverent awe. This is what the writer of Proverbs meant when he said, "Fear the Lord" (Prov. 3:7). This does not mean to dread the Lord nor to cringe in his presence, but to stand in wonder and submission before his holiness. It means to fear God so much that we need not fear anything else at all.

III. The final requirement for seeing God is to "depart from evil" (Prov. 3:7). The veil of sin hangs dark between his face and ours. Jesus said, "Blessed are the pure in heart: for they shall see God" (Matt. 5:8). Those whose singlehearted devotion to God leaves no place for the alloy of sin are the only persons to whom the face of God comes clearly through.

If only we could trust him, if only we could stand in reverent awe, if only our hearts were pure, we too could say with William Noel Hodgson:

> When in the blue dusk of a summer night
> I watch God's largess of his silver stars,
> Sometimes, it seems, the adamantine bars
> Fall from the tall gates of the Infinite;

And time stands waiting. Then I seem to hear
As one who listens from a lonely height
To waters breaking on an unknown sea,
The strong pulse of the world-heart throbbing
near.
The mists roll back, and for a space stand clear
The great white windows of eternity.

## 17. What It Means to Be Saved

Nenien C. McPherson, Jr.

•

Many men say that sin is an old-fashioned word that no longer
has meaning. We have complexes and repressions, phobias and
neuroses. We make mistakes and are selfish, greedy, and even
unkind, but sin, we conclude, is an outmoded concept. And yet,
having said all this, most of us are conscious of a deep-seated
sense of misdirection. Like the Apostle Paul, we are well aware
that "when I want to do right, evil lies close at hand" (Rom.
7:21, RSV).

So also with salvation. We are sometimes offended by what
we call the "old-time" preaching which seems otherworldly,
narrowly negative, and makes salvation an escape from a future
damnation. We forget that salvation is a word having a positive
as well as the negative meaning.

Salvation means deliverance from sinful habits and selfish
ways, freedom from fear, anxiety, and a sense of the futility of
life, and the dissolving of our prejudices and sense of guilt.
But, even more, salvation means to be saved to something and
for something. Jesus said, "I came that they may have life, and
have it abundantly" (John 10:10, RVS). Salvation means the
attaining of fullness of life. This Tennyson declared in "The
Two Voices" is our need:

'Tis life whereof our nerves are scant,
O life, not death, for which we pant;
More life and fuller that I want.

And this Christ offers to men.

Life is more than existence. George Bernard Shaw once said that the epitaph for many people should read, "Died at thirty, buried at sixty." One may exist years after life and the relationships that make it worthwhile have lost their meaning. For life is a matter of relationships.

To be saved means to enter into right relations with God, with one's fellow men, with the world of things, and with oneself. The most important relationship and the one that determines all others is one's relationship to God. To enter into a right relationship with the Christ of love and gracious goodwill is a transforming experience that comes only as a man recognizes his need and is willing to be changed.

I. The first step is the surrender of pride and an acknowledgment of one's dependence upon a power beyond himself. In the Garden of Eden the first man and woman succumbed to the promise of independence from God: "You will be like God" (Gen. 3:5, RSV). Then they would need no power beyond themselves.

Alcoholics Anonymous is built on the principle that the first step toward sobriety is to acknowledge that one's life has become unmanageable and that in his own power a man cannot stop drinking. Admitting this, he turns his life over to God. The individual who will not take this first step cannot be helped. This is as true of other sinful habits as that of drinking.

The Prodigal Son's sins were primarily of the flesh, but those of the Elder Brother, pride and self-righteousness, were no less deadly. Deliverance from the sin of pride is not easy and can be done only by finding a new center for life and experiencing the expulsive power of a new affection and a new loyalty.

II. The second step in entering into a right relationship with God through Christ is to repent of one's sins. The Greek word *"metanoia,"* which is much stronger than "repentance" and "remorse," means to change one's mind, to make a positive about-face, and to move in a new direction.

Humility and repentance are themselves products of God's Spirit working in and on our spirits, "For by grace you have been saved through faith; and this is not your own doing, it is the gift of God—not because of works, lest any man should boast" (Eph. 2:8-9, RSV). Our redemption comes when we accept God's gracious offer of forgiveness and help through faith and trust in him which is itself a gift of God. Then we willingly forsake our prideful sense of self-sufficiency because we have discovered we cannot change ourselves, we acknowledge our wrong-being and wrong-doing and move in a new direction, and we accept in humble trust God's offer to forgive and accept us, not because of what we are, but because of his Christlike, gracious goodwill.

III. A right relationship with God inevitably leads to a right relationship with our fellow men and the world of things. We begin to see as God sees and care as God cares. His spirit of love dissolves our blind spots and prejudices so that we love all men without regard to color of skin or their status in society. In brief, to be a Christian means to have the mind of Christ and to permit his spirit of love to determine our attitudes and responses in every area. No man can be saved without entering into a right relationship with man as well as with God. Jesus says, "If you are offering your gift at the altar, and there remember that your brother has something against you, leave your gift there before the altar and go; first to be reconciled to your brother, and then come and offer your gift" (Matt. 5:23-24, RSV).

Things also fall into their proper place when this new relationship has been established. We see ourselves as stewards of God's graciousness and not as owners, and we use all we have as his servants.

God continuously comes to all of us with an offer of help, but there is always a demand that we give our supreme loyalty to him. So salvation means entering into a right relationship with Christ, which is really a gift from God to which we respond in humble trust and faith, and into a right relationship with our fellow men, material things, and ourselves.

## 18. Salvation for the Lost Condition

HORACE BUSHNELL

•

For the Son of man is come to save that which was lost. MATTHEW 18:11

Every kind of work supposes something to be done, some ground or condition of fact to be affected by it; education the fact of ignorance, punishment the fact of crime, charity the fact of want. The work of Christ, commonly called a work of salvation, supposes in like manner the fact of a lost condition, such as makes salvation necessary. So it is that Christ himself conceives it, "For the Son of man is come to save that which is about to be, or in danger of being, lost," but he uses the past tense, *"was lost,"* as if it were a fact already consummated, or, at least, practically determined. This work, therefore, is to be a salvation, not as being a preventive, but as being a remedy after the fact; a supernatural provision by which seeds of life are to be ingenerated in a lapsed condition where there are none. At this point then Christianity begins. This is the grand substructural truth on which it rests, that man who is to be saved by it, is a lost being—already lost.

And this is salvation, the entering of the soul into God's divine order; for nothing is in order that is not in God, having God flow through it by his perfect will, even as he sways to unsinning obedience the tides of the sea, and the rounds of the stars. As we are lost men when lost to God, so we find ourselves when we find God. And then, how consciously do the soul's broken members coalesce and meet in Christ's order, when

Christ liveth in them. In this new relationship, the spirit of love and of a sound mind, all strength, free beauty, solid vigor, get their spring—we are no more lost. All that is in God or Christ his Son, flows in upon us—wisdom, righteousness, sanctification, redemption. We are new men created in righteousness after God. Even so, "in righteousness"; for we are new-charactered in God, closeted, so to speak, in God's perfections—in that manner justified, as if we had never sinned, justified by faith. We have put on righteousness of God, which is by faith of Jesus Christ, unto all and upon all them that believe.

This is the salvation that our God is working in his Son, but as the great apostle here intimates, it is, and is to be, by faith; for the result can never be issued save as we, on our part, believe. The very plan, or mode, of his working supposes a necessity of faith in us. For as God comes nigh us in his Son, he can be a salvation, only as we come nigh responsively to him, yielding our feeling to the cogent working of his. And this we do in faith. Faith is the act by which one being confides in another, trusting himself to that other, in what he is and undertakes. And there is nothing that puts a man so close to another's feeling, principle, and character as this act of trust. When you put such faith in a man, his opinions, ways, and even accents of voice have a wonderfully assimilative power in you. It is as if your life were overspread by his, included in his. To be nigh a great good mind, accepted in trust and friendship, is, in this manner, one of the greatest possible advantages, and especially so for a young person. In this fact you have the reason of that faith in Christ which is made the condition of salvation. For it is even your chance of salvation, as a lost man, that a being has come into the world, so great in character and feeling, that turning to be with him, he shall be in you. And therefore his apostle says, Christ, "is the power of God unto salvation to every one that believeth" (Rom. 1:16); and he himself, "He that believeth . . . shall be saved" (Mark 16:16). He can be no sufficient power, work no principle of life, save as he is welcomed to the heart by faith. In the same way, he calls you to "come," for coming is faith. And when he says, "Come unto me, all ye that labour and are heavy laden, and I will give you rest" (Matt. 11:28), he does not speak, as many think, to such as are only afflicted, world-sick, tired, pining in weak self-sympathy, but to them who are weary of their own evils, tossed and rent by their own disorders, thrown out of rest by the tumult of their thoughts and bosom troubles, starving in their own deep wants, crushed by their felt disabilities to good—in a word, lost men. Thus he speaks to you. And you come when you truly believe in him. Then you rest, rest in God's harmony, rest in peace—knowing in the blissful revelation of fact, how much it means that the Son of man is come to save that which was lost.

## 19. Marks of Sonship

DONALD GREY BARNHOUSE

•

As many as received him, to them gave he power to become the sons of God, even to them that believe on his name. JOHN 1:12

The fact that we can call ourselves sons of God is a miracle of God's great love to us. Love that goes upward from the heart of man to God is adoration. Love that goes outward, from one heart to another, is affection. Love that stoops is grace.

God stooped to us. For us, this is the most stupendous fact of the universe. It reveals to us that our God is love. We cannot find love in the forces of nature. There may be plan and determination, order and intelligence, but you cannot find love. There is nothing in the movements of the millions of suns that fleck the universe, nothing within the range of telescope or microscope that indicates love in nature. We cannot put love into a test tube, measure it with a micrometer, synthetize or analyze it. Love is not to be found in the forces of nature.

But God has demonstrated his love. When we were dead in trespasses and sins, he came—not clinging to the brightness of his glory, not shunning our lowly condition, but taking upon himself the form of a servant in the likeness of men. And that was not all. "Being found in fashion as a man, he humbled himself, and became obedient unto death, even the death of the cross" (Phil. 2:8). Now I know that God is not some far-distant, impersonal force. Now I know that God is love.

Do you have that supernatural life within you? Are you certain that you have been born again? Have you looked away to the Cross of Jesus Christ and found there the payment for your sin and the provision for your eternal righteousness?

Upon those who have thus believed, God puts the marks of sonship. What are these marks of sonship? What does God expect from those whom he has called to be sons and titled as his heirs?

I. The first mark of sonship is the right to become a son of God. Many who speak of the Fatherhood of God are either stealing a privilege that they know is not theirs, or they are deceived into believing that they have a privilege which has never been granted them. "But as many as received him, to them gave he power to become the sons of God, even to them that believe on his name."

II. The first mark of sonship is the right, the authority, to be a son of God and to call him Father. What do I say? Call him Father? Yes, that is the second mark of sonship. We have received the authority to be sons; we receive the right to call him Father. It was not always so. You do not find any suggestion of this privilege in the Old Testament. Our relationship to God as sons depended upon the work which Christ accomplished at the Cross of Calvary.

# III
# THE CALL
# TO DISCIPLESHIP

## 20. What It Means to Be a Christian

PAUL QUILLIAN

•

They took knowledge of them, that they had been with Jesus. ACTS 4:13

Discipleship in the days of the New Testament was clear and unmistakable—no great arguing about how one must be baptized, no detailed controversies over what doctrines one must believe in. To be a disciple of Jesus meant to believe in what Jesus did. For was he not the one sent of God, the interpreter of life, who came showing men the way, the truth, and the life?

Our personalities are made up of convictions and desires and actions. One can have convictions that are Christlike, but if his desires or his actions are not Christlike, he is not worthy to be called a Christian. Or one could have a wishful attitude toward the things which Christ desired, but if he did not have the convictions Jesus had, or if he did not follow his desires with an action that was consonant with his profession, he could not be called a Christian. Or if he, puppetlike, simply went through the activities that Christ went through, and had neither the desire nor the conviction that Christ had, he could not be called a Christian. But if one believes what Christ believed and one desires what Jesus desired and one seeks to do what Jesus did and taught other people to do, we do not need to look at the name above the church where he worships; we do not need to study the ritual he follows. A person who has taken Jesus as a worthy interpreter of life and put his whole personality into Jesus' keeping, whose convictions, desires, and activities are in harmony with his—that person is a disciple of Jesus.

Someone has said that Jesus played his life like music that was meant to be played over again. When Beethoven created a symphony, he did not write it that men should sit down before it and say, "How admirable!" He composed it so the music, having been created, could be played over and over again until men's hearts could be lifted from the low to the high, from despair to rejoicing. Just so Jesus with his faith in God, with his reverence for personality, with his devotion to justice, truth, and brotherhood. Just so Jesus lived his life, not for us to stand before others and say, "How lovely," but that the spirit of his life might be incarnated over and over again, played upon every human instrument until the orchestra of life should take up the strain, bringing joy to God, who created the players.

Who knows what music the organ of our life can produce if the fingers of the living Christ play upon the keyboard, if discipleship means for us what it meant for the early Christians —namely, to believe what Jesus believed, to desire what Jesus desired, to seek to do what Jesus did and taught other people to do?

## 21. The Dread of Being Chosen

ROBERT G. MIDDLETON

•

And when he heard this, he was very sorrowful. LUKE 18:23

"When Christ calls a man," said Dietrich Bonhoeffer, "he bids him come and die." Confronted with a demand so rigorous, it is not surprising that there should be a dread of being chosen. Such a call leads us into the depths, and we prefer the shallows; it summons us to a task, and we prefer to explore ideas; it demands everything, and we want to offer fragments. Hence it is that so many, aware of the radical nature of the call of Christ, prefer not to hear it. They employ all sorts of strategies to escape this confrontation by the disturbing Christ. And in the process their faith remains unsatisfying, lacking in joy and abandon, a tame and drab affair.

There are many strategies for escaping the hazard of being chosen. We can wrap ourselves in religious activities, using these as a cushion to deaden the impact of the living God. Even our religious beliefs can be hiding places from God. Forsaking the Biblical witness of the God who lays his hand in imperious summons upon men, we fashion our own idea of a God who understands the frailty of our human nature and does not make impossible demands of us. Because this dread of being chosen is so powerful in us, there are many who use unbelief as a shield to protect them from the inexorable summons of God.

The result of these strategies is that we, like the Rich Young Ruler, turn away "sorrowful." To be chosen is too much for us. It is, perhaps, hard for us to imagine that men have this dread of God. Honesty, however, compels our assent to the assertion of Paul Tillich who says that "man desires to escape God. . . . Men of all kinds, prophets and reformers, saints and atheists, believers and unbelievers, have the same experience. It is safe to say that a man who has never tried to flee God has never experienced the God who is really God." Hosts of men have been "sorrowful" when they have faced the demand of Christ.

I. This dread of being chosen roots in the fact that to be chosen by God means the acceptance of tension. All of us have a desire, secret or open, to make our peace with this world. There is something in man which makes it distasteful always to be fighting things. Because it is so plainly a fact that the choice of Christ is also the choice of tension, men try to make an adroit compromise with the world. In the abandonment of this tension, men think they will find peace. Torn apart by the tension between the vision of Christ's way and the world's blatant refusal of that way, we find release only by escaping the choice, thus purchasing a superficial ease, but always troubled because we sense that we have rejected the Truth for the world's illusion, the Way for the world's chaos, the Life for the world's death. Or—and this is the other option before us— we can accept the tension, bearing it gladly, thus helping to share the sufferings of our Lord and finding that this tension is itself part of the Cross we as Christians must be willing to bear.

II. There is this dread of being chosen because it means the abandonment of independence. This is near the heart of what it means to have faith. We are no longer in command of ourselves; we are under orders, waiting upon God in eager faith and glad obedience. It is this unconditional surrender which makes and marks the Christian. To be a Christian, in Emil Brunner's blunt language, means that we take ourselves by the scruff of the neck and hurl ourselves off the throne in the center and place Christ there. This is what conversion means, and this is why it is always so dramatic and even devastating an experience. It is a revolution—nothing less.

We do not really understand ourselves until we recognize how fiercely we resist this surrender. For the heart of our human predicament is that we are proud and self-centered. To escape this predicament is never an easy experience, nor a gradual transition. It is death to self in order to live to God. Fiercely clinging to our independence, we turn away "sorrowful," knowing that we cannot find real freedom except in bondage to God. Yet we resist with stubbornness such a surrender.

III. The dread of being chosen roots also in the fact that it means the assumption of burdens. When God chooses us, he confers upon us the privilege of sharing one another's burdens. We are from that moment on bound to our fellow human beings by the ties of love and compassion.

This acceptance of a burden is always the result of the God-given choice of a man. This choice sent Trevor Huddleston to Africa, there to bear witness in the shantytowns of Johannesburg to God's love for the native people. This choice sent Dietrich Bonhoeffer to Nazi Germany, there to end his life on a gallows. To be a Christian is to accept the burden of the world's anguish and woe.

To be a Christian is not to choose an easy path nor a conventional and prosaic goodness. It is to live with tension, to accept bondage to God, and to assume the burdens of men. It is, in short, what seems to be death, but it is always the way to life eternal and abundant.

## 22. The Demands of Discipleship

MASSEY MOTT HELTZEL

•

If any man will come after me, let him deny himself, and take up his cross, and follow me. MATTHEW 16:24

Jesus had just told his disciples that he must go to Jerusalem and suffer. Those who came after him would have to travel a similar road. He saw what he would have to do; they must see what they would have to do. The conditions of messiahship were clear; the conditions of discipleship must be made clear. It would be costly to him to fulfill his mission; it could be costly to them to fulfill their mission. This was the way the Master chose; should not the servant choose it still? Discipleship demands self-denial, cross-bearing, and loving obedience.

There is a second demand. "If any man will come after me, let him . . . take up his cross." The disciples knew only too well what this meant. A condemned man was required to carry his own cross, or at least the cross beam, to the place of execution. No doubt most of the disciples had seen more than one man pick up a cross and walk through the village streets, never to come back. They knew that taking up a cross meant making the supreme sacrifice. The first Christians certainly did this, and the devout servants of the Church through all the Christian centuries have done it. The pertinent question is, Have we done it?

We may say that we are carrying a cross when we are not doing so at all. We may bear a burden or endure a thorn, but we do not often take up a cross. A burden is the inevitable load which life lays upon every man. A thorn is the sharp affliction which in some form most people must bear. A cross is our voluntary self-denial for Christ's sake. "The burden and the thorn are universal, and they are inescapable," W. M. Clow wrote. "But the cross is not universal, and the cross can be escaped. Many men and women never bear a cross at all. . . . Your cross is something you can take or you can refuse."

A cross is not some heavy duty which you must face, not some terrible temptation which eats into your character, not some sorrow, some loss, and not what Shakespeare's Hamlet would call

The slings and arrows of outrageous fortune

*

and the thousand natural shocks
That flesh is heir to.

A cross is something which you deliberately take up for the sake of Christ and also something which you could avoid if you were not desirous of putting him first in your life. When, with no one twisting your arm, you throw yourself into the struggle against evil, that is taking up your cross. When you do something for Christ and the Church which you know will cause you to be misunderstood, opposed, criticized, and disliked, that is taking up your cross. When you speak out against some custom which you consider pagan and sinful and when, by remaining silent, you could be thought of as a "good fellow," that is taking up your cross. When you stop doing something which you have done for years and your friends pommel you with questions and imply that you are foolish or narrow-minded and you reply that you changed because you came to know Christ better and to understand discipleship more fully, that is taking up your cross. When you witness, in an unfriendly atmosphere, to the saving power of his death and resurrection, that is taking up your cross.

Jesus says that we cannot come after him until we do take up something which we do not have to take up. Will we, then, act when we could evade, simply because we feel that as modern disciples we ought to take sides? Will we oppose things which we consider evil—traditions, business and social practices—because we are convinced that following Christ demands it? This text puts it bluntly: there is no discipleship without cross-bearing.

This is hard doctrine for the present age. We have removed discipline from church membership; we have gone out of our way to make the Christian life seem easy; and now we can hardly believe that Jesus would expect of us all that we have said. But the unwelcome fact is that he expects even more. The eminent essayist John Ruskin once wrote that the Christian Church has turned the Cross from a gallows into a raft, and there is no use in trying to escape the bite of his words. We almost make the text read, "If any man will come after me, he shall have smooth sailing."

Discipleship is demanding; Christ is a stern Commander; our Lord is imperious in his claims upon us. But—and this is gospel—discipleship is also rewarding, for Jesus continued, "Whosoever will save his life shall lose it: and whosoever will lose his life for my sake shall find it" (Matt. 16:25).

## 23. On Being Involved

WESLEY P. FORD

•

But seek first his kingdom and his righteousness. MATTHEW 6:33, RSV

"By being involved in an event," states the existentialist, "and by exercising decision one really exists." A major decision concerns the level at which to be involved. One may exist while playing at little games, but given sensitivity and freedom, one may choose to be involved at a high level. Jesus chose to struggle toward what he believed would achieve the maximum quality of life for all mankind. For him the choice was not simple assent; it was a costly way of life. For us the decision to follow Christ is not just one among many decisions; it is a choice that affects all other decisions we make.

To choose high-level involvement requires self-denial. We cannot serve the cause of the high road while clinging to the fruits of the low road. Some things must be put down, if others would be lifted up. Ruskin said, "If you read this, you cannot read that." Jesus had power to do with; he also had power to do without. "If any man would come after me, let him deny himself" (Matt. 16:24, RSV).

I. Why pay the price of self-denial to be involved at the high level of allegiance to Christ? There are many reasons. One is that we are constantly surrounded by the temptation to evil or to second best. We need constantly to be confronted by the temptation to be good. We are neither as good as we ought to be, nor as good as we know how to be. Why? Who will deliver us? A man said of Socrates, "There is one experience I have in the presence of this man alone such as nobody would expect of me, and that is to be made to feel ashamed; he alone can make me feel it. . . . As soon as I turn from his company I fall victim to the favors of the crowd." Each will be a better person if he walks in the presence of one who makes him feel ashamed, who tempts him to be good. This Jesus Christ does.

II. A second reason for commitment to Christ is our need for the compulsion of a worthy purpose. Unless one comes to life with a sense of direction and with his mind made up about something, he is victimized by circumstances. The Christian life at best is focused on goals so compelling that its urgency determines circumstances. Mastered by the compulsion of the kingdom, Jesus found his way through every man-made labyrinth or barrier. Compelled by Christ, Paul knew he must go to Rome, Tyndale knew he must translate the Bible, and Livingstone knew he must go to Africa. Each of these, driven by great purpose, pushed circumstances aside and walked through overwhelming odds to reach his goal.

III. A third reason for commitment to Christ is what our choice does for others. The followers of Christ, the seekers of the kingdom, keep alive the hope for, and the discipline that will make possible, a better day. We may shrug our shoulders at such counsel as "Love your enemies, do good to those who hate you" (Luke 6:27) and "Blessed are the meek" (Matt. 5:5), but may God be merciful to us if the day ever comes when such great insights no longer disturb and goad us. We commit our lives to the Lordship of Jesus Christ, aware that the society in which and by which we live cannot endure unless haunted by the ideals he espoused.

To live is to be involved. To live most usefully is to be involved in behalf of the highest; therefore, we surrender ourselves to Jesus Christ, aware that we need the temptation to be good, the compulsion of great purpose, and the discipline and the hope of the kingdom which he sought.

## 24. The Silence of Unutterable Things

PERCY C. AINSWORTH

•

I have yet many things to say unto you, but ye cannot bear them now. JOHN 16:12

*"I . . . but ye . . . ."* That is ever the sad antithesis that explains the ignorance of human hearts concerning things divine. We say, "Why has not this or that been revealed unto us? Why in such and such a thing have we been left in darkness?" The darkness is not above us, but within us. The reticence of heaven is only the weakness and unworthiness of the human heart viewed, so to speak, from above. There is always a silence at the heart of speech. Sometimes it is the silence born of the speaker's limited knowledge; sometimes, as in this case of Jesus and his disciples, it is the silence born of the hearers' limited power of reception and response. Jesus kept back nothing that his disciples were able to receive. He could not speak because they could not hear. He told them less than he knew, but as much as they were able to know.

His reticence was not arbitrary. It was perfectly congruous to the whole law and principle of revelation. The great problem of the prophet and the preacher has ever been the unprepared heart of the people. Willingness to listen is not always equivalent to ability to understand. And if the small distance that lies between the wisest and the most foolish man counts for so much, if we in our human experience know how even a slight advance beyond our fellows in knowledge or sensitiveness can seal our lips, or at any rate limit our utterance, how much more should the Eternal Word be folded about with a silence conditioned by the darkness of men's minds and the hardness of their hearts! Jesus could not have taught the world as much as he did teach it had he not chosen out of it just a few souls who by their history, nature, and affinities were comparatively teachable. And even these he could not teach just as he would. That which seemed complete to them was fragmentary to him. They counted him to have said all when there was yet all to say. He was always sounding their thoughts and hopes and sympathies. And, alas! many a thought of his he dared not launch because it would straightway have gone aground, and have been stranded and useless in the shallows of their lives.

Revelation is not mechanical; it is moral. One of the great ends of life is to make us able to know. Experience does not make us wise merely by the measure of the experience itself; it is meant so to affect our character that we may be put into touch with some further range of that divine truth that is ever waiting at the door of our hearts. Experience by itself cannot make us wise, but it can make us teachable.

And revelation is progressive. "Ye cannot bear them *now*," said Jesus of the things he wished to teach his disciples. They were able to receive them by and by. They became in time able to know. The knowledge of spiritual things is not in any man's life a matter distinct and separate from all else. It is bound up with his reverence, courage, love, and faithfulness; and as these things grow in him, so does one and another of the "many things" pass into his life's possession.

## 25. God Pursuing the Soul

### R. J. CAMPBELL

•

There is something almost awful in this thought of a pursuing God, "this tremendous Lover" as Francis Thompson calls him, a God who will not let us alone but follows us up with pain and disillusionment while ever we seek our good in anything that keeps us from him. We think we are seeking God, but it is far truer to say that he is seeking us and that we are continually trying to run away from him. We cannot find him by any exercise of human wisdom, nor is a merely intellectual homage what he wants; he wants the soul, stripped of all lesser attachments, and he means to get it, however hard he may have to hurt in order to attain his end. He is a fierce lover, is God, relentless, unyielding, persistent, invincible, and yet of limitless tenderness and a sweet kindness inexhaustible. Who so terrible as God, yet who so wooingly gentle when he has gained possession of the soul!

Look at your own life. How has God been treating you?

Is there no one now within range of my voice who was once well on the road to being a frivolous, contemptible, ignoble character, and was saved from that horrible fate by the shock of some overwhelming disaster or heart-rending sorrow? God took away from you the delight of your eyes, and in so doing rescued your soul from the pit of hell. I may be speaking to someone who has passed through an anguish so great that you wonder you ever survived it. How small to you now seem the objects on which you once set your heart! And is there no one here who has known what it is to be disappointed in life of nearly every object for which he has strenuously striven? The fruitless struggle after them has taught you something—you are the greater and stronger because of it—but to have gained them would have been no blessing. You see it now and do not regret the pain the vision has cost. God has a wonderful way of revealing himself to the soul that has suffered loss and is thereby detached from ephemeral quests and unsatisfying objects of desire. I have heard more than one truehearted man confess that they did not know how strong a hold this world had upon them until their deepest affections were shattered by bereavement or something worse—perhaps by cruel betrayal and desertion. Then the divine Lover laid mightily hold of them and gave them back to life in a purer, nobler spirit; henceforth they saw all mankind through an atmosphere of deep compassion and desiring to help. After a long chase, during which they had been trying all kinds of substitutes for the life eternal, God had seized their naked souls and bound them fast to himself forevermore.

God is hunting you through every false experience in which your soul seeks rest, tracking you down through sorrow after sorrow, driving you forth from everything unreal, that in the end he may gasp and hold you eternally, the willing prisoner of his love.

## 26. Why Should a Young Man Be a Christian?

JOHN WATSON

•

Thou hast the dew of thy youth. PSALM 110:3

There are reasons why of all people it is most fitting that a man in the flush of his youth should accept Christ, and why the religion of Jesus makes its most persuasive appeal to men in their early life.

And the reason I wish to urge this is because our Master was a young man. We are apt to forget that the supreme achievement in human history was wrought by One who never reached middle age, to forget how short was Christ's public life, and how soon it was closed. At an age when people are beginning to consider other young men, and to prophesy that they will do something before they die, this Man had closed his career and completed his work. It was not an old man worn by long years, and weary with the toil of life, and separated by a gulf from the enthusiasms of youth who died so gloriously upon the Cross—it was a Man in the perfection of strength, with a body of superb endurance, and a soul triumphant over circumstances.

Within less than three years our Master fulfilled his commission and returned it to God. Within that brief time, during which he never wrote a word, he made a larger contribution to human thought than all the books that ever have been printed. He did more for the good of the human race than all the martyrs, reformers, prophets, and apostles who have lived before and after him, and he changed the direction and the issues of human history. A young man then, nineteen hundred years ago, and a young man still, who carries forever the freshness of his youth.

It was to young men Christ made his most pointed and direct appeals; with young men he succeeded and triumphed. Whatever may be the advantages worldly experience and ripe wisdom afford for business, for politics, for teaching, and for government—and perhaps the advantages are much overrated—religion seeks her recruits among those not yet old, assigns her greatest tasks to youth, and confers on youth her crown. It was a dozen young men, with another man still young, who joined them afterward, who revolutionized human thought, put a new face on human society, and founded a greater kingdom than the Roman Empire. They had not wealth, those twelve, nor position, nor learning, nor even wisdom, but they had the priceless and overflowing resources of youth, and this youth responded to the call of Christ, and gave itself to his great endeavor.

# IV
# BORN-AGAIN
# MEN

# 27. Born Again

STEPHEN W. PAINE

•

Verily, verily, I say unto thee, Except a man be born again, he cannot see the kingdom of God. JOHN 3:3

These surprising and somewhat peremptory words were uttered by a humble Galilean teacher named Jesus during the course of a friendly visit with an outstanding young leader of the Jewish people named Nicodemus, who had gone out of his was to pay a courteous call to the little-known Galilean, who was said to be working miracles of divine power.

Surprising and unexpected as were these mystic words about being "born again" or "born from above," as the Greek permits, they spoke to a real need in Nicodemus' mind and heart. He had much to make him respected and even envied. He was a churchman and a Pharisee. The Pharisees were most loyal to the worship of Jehovah, the laws of Moses, and the traditional observances of the Jewish religion. So Nicodemus may be said to have been a spiritual leader of his generation.

Nicodemus was also a political leader or "ruler," actually a member of the Jewish senate or council of seventy called the Sanhedrin. He was learned, a "master [or teacher] of Israel." He was wealthy, as is indicated by his later providing costly spices for Jesus' burial (see John 19:39). He was courteous and fine in his manner, addressing the man from the uncouth north

75

country with respect, "Master" or "Rabbi"—our equivalent to "Reverend" or "Doctor"—even as he himself was wont to be addressed.

But despite all his talents and assets, this young churchman had come to Jesus with an inner need. And Jesus recognized the need with that divine insight which enabled him to read the very thoughts of men. Making use of the "shock-therapy" approach which he knew so well, he gently brushed aside the gentilities of the situation and opened up the real question, What must a man do to inherit "eternal life" or the "kingdom of God"?

The "kingdom of God" was the topic of much discussion. To the Jews of that day it was a utopian dream closely bound up with God's promise of a national deliverer from the family of David. The "kingdom of heaven," it was generally thought, would be an earthly situation involving for the Jewish people a joy springing from ideal outer circumstances. These were to include the restoration of Israel's national freedom and the establishment of her supremacy as a world power as well as boundless material blessings both national and personal. For those closest to the prince, "the kingdom" would also mean great individual power and prestige (see Matt. 19:27; 20:21).

Man in all ages has, of course, told himself that if only he might have ideal surroundings, he would be happy. Plato's *Republic* set forth a state in which life would be ideal because the people would be ruled by philosophy and a philosopher-king. Thomas More's *Utopia* anticipated that man's condition would be blessed through right education. Francis Bacon's *New Atlantis* proposed a life of happiness through the scientific conquest of nature. Hitler's Third Reich was to be a utopia of racial supremacy. Karl Marx proposed a proletarian utopia through the abolition of faulty bourgeois morality and the establishment through world revolution of a classless society.

Nor should we pass by the unabashedly materialistic panaceas, whether proposed by politicians or dreamed by private citizens, current in our own wealthy land. How convinced we seem to be that a man's life does consist in his possessions and that happiness is insured by social security, crop supports, split-level houses, new cars, and power boats. All of these schemes have been tried or are being tried as avenues to happiness, although testimony may be amassed to any desired extent declaring their futility. Sooner or later every man takes his place beside the wealthy, gifted, and popular Nicodemus.

What, then, does Christ propose? A happiness based upon a radical change, not of our circumstances, but of ourselves. "Ye must be born again" (John 3:7).

To Nicodemus, in his failure to comprehend the spiritual application of this figure, Jesus explains that this is not a physical matter, but a spiritual regeneration marked by that deep-seated repentance for sin. This was the burden of John the Baptist's message, symbolized by the water so well known for its place in John's ministry. Here, then, is a birth "of water and of the Spirit." Not only is the negative condition of repentance implied, but also the positive supernatural act of God the Holy Spirit in the reorientation of a previously self-centered life.

Now Jesus proceeds to relate this supernatural new birth to his coming crucifixion (see John 3:14-15; 12:32-33). He finally brings the conversation to the requirement of personal faith in himself (John 3:16-17). A loving but just Father has given his Son, so that whoever puts full trust in that Son escapes destruction and finds that life of the ages and that inner rebirth which is in itself the kingdom of God. This was later to be the message, the "good news," of the Christian Church. The Apostle Paul summarized its requirements as "repentance toward God, and faith toward our Lord Jesus Christ" (Acts 20:21).

How often has it been our privilege as Christians to point lost happiness-hunters to him who said, "I am the way, the truth, and the life: no man cometh unto the Father, but by me" (John 14:6)? Often there has come to us a seeker who in an incredulous half-skepticism says, "It can't possibly be this simple." At times, knowing some of the serious involvements, we too have been tempted to say, "Will God, can God, do it for even this one?" But when sincere and godly sorrow for sin merges into simple appropriating faith in the validity of Christ's sacrifice and of his promise, "Him that cometh to me I will in no wise cast out" (John 6:37), the miracle never fails of repetition; a soul is "born from above" or "born anew," and a changed life begins its unfolding.

## 28. Except a Man Be Born Again

GORDON POWELL

•

Jesus answered . . . Except a man be born again, he cannot see the kingdom of God. JOHN 3:3

When we enter the new life at the spiritual level God himself is our father. Where Paul refers to the "new creature" (2 Cor. 5:17), the margin of the New English Bible translates it "a new act of creation." Moffatt in his translation of the third chapter of John keeps the "born from above" thought throughout. Billy Graham emphasizes that when Jesus talked about being born again the verb is always passive. It is not something we can do for ourselves. We can and must create the conditions by true repentance, but in the end rebirth is essentially the gift of God. It is by water and the Spirit.

Like many of the rest of us, Nicodemus found this point difficult. So Jesus began to talk about the wind. I like the suggestion that the place where they met was the Garden of Gethsemane and the wind was rustling in the olive trees. Now it so happens that both in the Hebrew and in the Greek the word for wind and the word for spirit are one and the same (*ruach* in Hebrew and *pneuma* in Greek). Jesus used this to bring home to Nicodemus the reality of the Divine Spirit. Nicodemus did not doubt the wind he could hear with his ears, though he had no idea where it came from or whither it was going. In the same way we may not be able to explain the workings of the Spirit of God, but all around us we can see the results in born-again lives.

Sometimes the wind of the Spirit blows softly and gently over many years to effect the miracle of the new birth; sometimes it blows with great force to bring about a dramatic change in a human personality within a few minutes. We must not think that because we have never had a tumultuous emotional experience that we have been denied the Second Birth as some quite saintly people have sometimes thought. Over the total picture there is probably a higher percentage of lasting conversions when the Second Birth has extended over a period than when it has been sudden. We have all seen trees which have been bent by the wind. No sudden gale has been responsible, but prevailing winds blowing for a very long time.

Even when the turning point appears sudden the full experience often requires months, perhaps years.

You may say, "I would like to have this new life. I can see the need to repent and it would be wonderful to receive the gift of the Spirit. I have often repented of my sin, but I don't receive the assurance of salvation or any sense of power. What lack I yet?"

The answer is "Believe on the Lord Jesus Christ" (Acts 16:31). In the twelfth verse of his Gospel John has written, "As many as received him, to them gave he power to become the sons of God [to be born again spiritually by God], even to them that believe on his name" (John 1:12). Belief to be effective must involve every part of the personality. There must be belief in the mind, with the intellect. There must be an emotional response. When we love Christ then all the forces of the personality are focused, the conflicts are resolved, and we have a new sense of power if only because our own human resources are released. As Professor Jung put it, "It is the incapacity to love which robs man of his possibilities." But Christ revives this capacity. He is the supreme object of our love. When we prove our love in the way love must always prove itself, by joyful obedience of the will, then we rediscover the ancient truth, "Where love is, there life begins." Rebirth happens when we believe in and receive him who said, "I am come that they might have life, and that they might have it more abundantly" (John 10:10).

## 29. How?

### SAMUEL M. SHOEMAKER

●

Except a man be born again, he cannot see the kingdom of God. Nicodemus saith unto him, How . . . ? JOHN 3:3-4

Nicodemus began by recognizing Christ's power, "We know that thou art a teacher come from God: for no man can do these miracles that thou doest, except God be with him." He didn't really get to his point before Christ cut in with something that took the direction of the conversation. "Except a man be born again, he cannot see the kingdom of God." That was not administration, or code, or institutionalism: that was experience. And that was where Nicodemus was weak. It is where all his lineal descendants—the cultivated, well-intentioned, inarticulate, diffident, institution-minded laymen, and clergymen—are weak today. "Ye must be born again." But generally their "must" is that they "must" look after the family income, or they "must" keep the religious institution going.

They are always uneasy when anybody comes to the question of experience. They don't quite think it is nice to talk about it. People like themselves have their religious code. Isn't that enough? And Christ simply says, not to the prodigals and sinners who already know that they need to be changed, but to the religious, the respectable, the church people, clergymen and pious laymen, "Except a man be born again, he cannot see the kingdom of God." It is difficult for a person like this to see where he needs anything more. He believes in the Commandments, he says his prayers, he is a good, religious citizen—what more *can* Jesus Christ want of him? For, mind you, Nicodemus was already just about everything that the present-day Christian Church requires of a layman. But still Christ says there is more to come. "Ye must be born again." All the poor bewildered man can say to him is, "How . . . ?" Nicodemus knew the "what" of religion, but he didn't know its "how." People like him can tell you everything about religion; the only thing they fail in is in telling you how you find it. A whole present-day world stands there with Nicodemus before Jesus Christ, and asks that question. There is nothing wrong with the content of Christianity; there is almost everything wrong with its presentation by the Christian Church today.

If the Christian Church is to be effective again in the affairs of men, it must begin by once more illuminating this great truth of rebirth. We must see it, not in the light of somebody's extravagant religious enthusiasm; but in the light of a world trying to live without God at all, reduced to its own power and wisdom. We tend to relegate such a truth to a few emotional people, in special need, and rather susceptible; but Nicodemus was not from a slum. He was educated, he was balanced, he was privileged—and Christ told him he needed a new birth.

*A man is born again when the control of his life, its center and its direction, pass from himself to God.* We can go to church for years without having that happen. You can easily be vaccinated with just enough dead germs of Christianity to make you immune to the real thing, so immune that you won't even know it when you see it. But then life and facts turn on us and make us face the truth. We look out on a world like ours; we helped make it, but we have no power to help remake it. We bleat plaintively or criticize censoriously; but in our hearts we know that something is desperately wrong, and we are part of the wrong. We may then be given grace to develop a conviction of sin. We who stand for God have helped the world away from him because we have not let him completely into our lives. What good to him or man is our respectability when dishonesty, greed, fear, conformity, meanness with our possessions, negative thinking, criticalness, uncleanness, above all our spiritual ineffectiveness, give the lie to our outward respectability? We shall begin knowing the need of a new birth when we begin knowing that it is the sins of people like you and me that have made this world into the hell it is today.

And the thing to do with sin is to do what Nicodemus did: go and search out someone with whom we can talk privately and frankly. Tell them of these things and, with them, to God. You say that you can do this alone with God; and I ask you, Have you succeeded in doing so? I said I was going to do that for years, but it never happened until I let a human witness come in on my decision. That is the "how" of getting rid of sin if you are in earnest about doing it at all: face it, share it, surrender it, hate it, forsake it, confess it, and restore for it.

## 30. Born Again

G. STANLEY RUSSELL

•

Jesus answered and said unto him . . . Except a man be born again, he cannot see. . . . JOHN 3:3

Christianity stands upon that affirmation of the Second Birth. Not upon the nature of God, however much the mystery intrigues us; not even upon the question of immortality, however deeply the futility or otherwise of existence be involved in it; least of all upon economics; but upon the necessity of being born again, our religion is established. It is the demand for a central, individual, transforming experience which renders the Gospel different from every other faith. Without that it would be possible to have a religion but impossible to prefix the adjective "Christian" to it. Never should that be more carefully remembered than when we are confronted by a disillusioned civilization.

Into such a world came Christianity—with not a word to say on what I have no doubt the wiseacres of the period designated as its "problems." Indeed, it had nothing to say on any subject save one—the necessity for being born again. All government, all economics, all business, all social relationships, waited on that for their redemption. If they could not impose that upon the world, Christians could and did impose it upon themselves, with the result that, out of all the institutions of the Roman Empire, the one survival today is the ever-threatened Church of Jesus. As Clement of Alexandria put it in the second century, "Christ hath turned sunset into sunrise"—and how? Simply by making men believe it was possible to see life steadily and see it whole only by being born of the spirit.

The world becomes, as Jesus said it was, unimportant alongside one's own soul. We determine upon God. Probably we begin with the religion of Jesus—the most God-conscious of all the pilgrims through the lanes of earth. Then from the religion *of* Jesus we pass inevitably to the religion *in* Jesus, and thence to its summit—the Cross. If you ask me whether life is worth living, I think I should reply that, without the Cross, I am not sure that it is. Take out of history the fact that the noblest and best humanity it ever contained paid the supreme price for an ideal, refused earthly crowns in the interests of victorious personality, and what rebuke remains to the greedy struggle that we call "getting on"? Indeed, the Cross stands in our midst to rescue us from cheap and easy notions of comfort, of divine favor and selfishness, as the truest wisdom. The ways of God are vindicated; we rise into a new world, with new values, new atmosphere, and new motives. We are "born again."

Well, and what is the result of a birth? A babe. Who shall tell us what that means? Who shall tell us what anything means that comes from God? A birth and a babe—they too are beyond us. Not even the poets can help us here. "Babes in Christ" (1 Cor. 3:1)—and we thought ourselves so wise.

We are experts in worldliness and we bring our technique to managing religion. That's why we make such a mess of it. Babes do not "manage" things; they break things. If we smashed our alabaster boxes over the feet of Christ and filled the house with the ointment, and gave up the election of Mr. Worldly Wiseman to the chief place in our synagogues, the Christian religion would begin to move—like an avalanche. But this prominent official is always suggesting that we must never be extravagant, never smash anything, always be prudent—things babes have never learned and have no business to know.

If you want to join the Church of Jesus Christ, don't get it into your head that you have to know all theology and all ethics, that you have to be good and to be able to present an unblemished record to the world. There comes from the new birth a babe—just beginning to live. You think yourself a very mature Christian. As a matter of fact you are just beginning to babble the heavenly speech, and to toddle in the direction of the door, and you will probably tumble several times before you reach it. Being a babe, you have got to know what there is through that door; you cannot rest until curiosity has been satisfied—and you stagger, and totter, and collapse more than once as you make your way to it. Well, you remember who said, "I am the door: by me if any man enter in, he shall be saved" (John 10:9). How wise that old hymn writer was—most of them are—who wrote, "I came to Jesus as I was." Then life begins; we are born into a new world; we see the kingdom of heaven and rejoice all our days, not only in that land of far-stretching distances, but in the King in his splendor, who is ours and whose we are.

## 31. The Will of the Wind

JOHNSTONE G. PATRICK

•

The wind blows where it wills. JOHN 3:8, NEB

"How is it possible," Nicodemus asked, "for a man to be born when he is old?" Preposterous! "Can he . . . ?" (John 3:4, NEB.) We all know by heart the conversation that took place on the moonlit night between the puzzled Pharisee and the under- standing Teacher. We remember each question and answer that led to the lovely and lively secret of spiritual renewal. The very idea of being "born over again" soared far beyond the mental reach of this ruler of the Jews, and perhaps Jesus paused at this point to ponder before the look of blank bewilderment upon his visitor's face.

Maybe, at the moment, a soft sighing of the night wind among some nearby olive trees could be heard. Jesus, who found so many of his inimitably haunting illustrations in the sounds, silences, and sights of the natural world, simply and shrewdly said, "The wind blows where it wills; you hear the sound of it"—listen!—"but you do not know where it comes from, or where it is going. So with everyone who is born from spirit."

Nicodemus knew next to nothing of the natural laws which govern the weather. Modern meteorology, however, has made us fairly familiar with cyclones and anticyclones, but, even so, the wind still symbolizes what we all, wittingly or unwittingly, most surely need. "The wind"—Christ's country-clean symbol of God's Spirit—"blows where it wills," and it is the will of the wind never to be still, but rather to blow always and everywhere.

> Hark to the wind how it blows!
> None comes, none goes,
> None reaps or mows,
> No friends turn foes,
> No hedge bears sloes,
> And no cock crows.
> But the wind knows.

"The wind knows," and that's why, to be sure, it "blows where it wills." God's Spirit knows there are needs to be met in every land and life, in every home and heart, and is always willing to meet each and all of them, in every shape and form, at all times and in all seasons, by day and night, in life and at death.

Jesus knew, too, and that's why he spoke of the greatest of all human needs, the necessity of a new birth, and a new life of love and liberty, but his flabbergasted inquirer, the needy Nicodemus, asked how such a miracle could happen, how such a wonder could be worked, and how there could ever be such a fresh start, such a thoroughgoing spiritual renewal, such an incredible change. It was the work of the willing Wind, God's Spirit, said Jesus, and everyone must experience what none can explain: the superabounding blessing of being "born over again." The wonder of God's Spirit, by means of the wonder of God's grace, is to operate on all levels of life, even on the lowest level, in the likeliest and unlikeliest of places, and for the neediest of God's children. It is like the wind! "The wind blows where it wills."

A proverb of the Scottish people, with a meaning above and beyond the natural, proclaims proudly, "The enemy may trample down the heather, but he cannot trample down the wind." The heather, though very tough and resilient, with difficulty may be trampled into the mud. But the wind cannot be trampled into the mud. In a short while the wind will rise, like the surprising Lord "with healing in his wings" (Mal. 4:2), and will fondle the poor trampled heather back into rare, rich, deep-purple beauty and will lift it again into life and loveliness.

Mankind everywhere, like the heather on the hills and "in the lonely hollows of the hills," has its enemies. At times, too, we need to be lifted from the mud in which we find ourselves mired by some fresh foe from without or an old enemy within. Let us not lose heart! "The enemy may trample down the heather, but he cannot trample down the wind." Listen! "The wind"—free, gloriously free—"blows where it wills." George Borrow's words still find a response: "There's night and day, brother, both sweet things; sun, moon, and stars, brother, all sweet things; there's likewise a wind on the heath."

A wind on the heath! Such is the free progress of God's Wind, carrying God's Word across the world. Like the wind upon the heath, it makes its spontaneous way over the face of the whole earth, bringing with it fresh faith and hope, "catching the trampled strands of truth, beauty, and love and lifting them into newness of life."

We do well to remind ourselves of what the Apostle Paul, from a stale, stuffy Roman cell, wrote in a letter to a young Lystrian lad. With shackles upon his wrists and depressing prison walls around him, ever the freest and sanest of men, he "sees life steadily and sees it whole," and he says, "Remember Jesus Christ, risen from the dead, born of David's line. This is the theme of my gospel, in whose service I am exposed to hardship, even to the point of being shut up like a common criminal; but the word of God is not shut up" (2 Tim. 2:8-9, NEB). What bracing good news! The enemies of Jesus and Paul had tried to trample down the heather, but they could not trample down the wind.

"Come wind, come weather." Can we, too, sing what the "avowed pilgrim," John Bunyan, sang, when the wind is God's Gracious, Truthful, Healthy, Holy Spirit? We most certainly can, for we, too, in the Will of the Wind, were meant to be "born over again" as sons and daughters of God.

"The wind blows where it wills." Listen! The Divine Breeze is blowing again our way.

> Breathe on me, Breath of God.
> Fill me with life anew.


## 32. Lives Remade

JOHN SUTHERLAND BONNELL

•

> Therefore, if any one is in Christ, he is a new creation; the old has passed away, behold, the new has come. 2 CORINTHIANS 5:17, RSV

The New Testament is a long record of changed lives—men and women who came into the presence of Christ and became changed personalities. At least twenty-eight personal interviews of Jesus are recorded in the brief compass of the Gospels. When we turn from the New Testament to the pages of Christian history, there is not a single century of our era that does not witness to some outstanding personality won to Christ, in addition to tens of thousands of less-celebrated persons. With some, the change was gradual; with others, it was spectacular and revolutionary. Let us consider three of these persons, all of whom tower above the men of their time.

I. The first is from the second half of the fourth century. Here is a young scholar, brilliant, winsome, profligate. In a garden at Milan he sheds tears of frustration and anguish: "O Lord, how long? how long? tomorrow and tomorrow and tomorrow? . . . Why not now? Why not this hour make an end of my weaknesses?" The sound of a voice breaks in upon his distress: "*Tolle lege. Tolle lege.*"—"Take up and read." Reaching for a copy of Paul's Epistles, he opens it and reads the words that first meet his eyes: "Let us conduct ourselves becomingly as in the day, not in reveling and drunkenness, not in debauchery and licentiousness, not in quarreling and jealousy. But put on the Lord Jesus Christ, and make no provision for the flesh, to gratify its desires" (Rom. 13:13-14, RSV). Then followed the miracle of inward renewal—and the Christian Church had found a mighty advocate in the great Augustine.

II. The scene changes to the thirteenth century in Italy. A group of well-to-do young men are making their way happily and boisterously through the streets of one of the hill towns. They are going to a banquet hall to do honor to the most popular youth in the town. His name is Giovanni and he is a born leader. At the height of the feast they crown him "King of Revelers." But in the midst of all the riotous celebration, Giovanni disappears. His friends are bewildered. They can find him nowhere. He has disappeared because even in the midst of all his riotous living a divine disquiet has laid hold of him. Now he must make his surrender to Christ. When his friends meet him again, he is totally changed. They find him devoting his life to prayer and to the service of the poor. So Giovanni became one of the most lovable characters of history and his example and preaching instituted a revival of religion in Italy and won the hearts of all men. This youth, Giovanni Francesco Bernardone, now grown into manhood, as brave as he was gentle and compassionate, is known to history as Francis of Assisi.

III. Finally, we turn to the twentieth century and see a young man nineteen years of age enrolling as an undergraduate at Oxford University. Before the year is over he has enlisted in the British army and is in the thick of the fighting in France. He is wounded and invalided to England. Now he is back again at Oxford. He has become a leader of the sophisticates, an emancipated, clever, cynical young agnostic. His chief joy is in casting sharp barbs of wit at Christians and Christianity. This brilliant youth has a large following among the students of Oxford, but the Hound of Heaven is on his trail. Twist and turn as he will, he knows that there is ultimately no escape. The crisis comes one night in Magdalen College. In his own bedroom he kneels in prayer and makes his commitment to Christ. Professor C. S. Lewis was recognized as one of the ablest defenders of Christianity in Britain. He labored to exalt the faith of Christ which he strove so long to destroy.

Evidence of the transforming power of Christ in human life ought to be manifest in every Christian church as a normal part of its work. There is no more powerful and compelling answer to the indifferent world than this: a spiritual dynamic enters into the hearts of men and women and changes them in the very depths of their being.

## 33. A Changed Life

### J. WILBUR CHAPMAN

•

Have you really taken all that God meant you should have? Your life is the test of this question. If you are constantly failing at the same point, if you are dominated by a spirit of unrest, if you are lacking in spiritual power, something is wrong and you need the touch of the living Christ.

The early disciples were an illustration of those of us who have not yet fully appreciated and appropriated our Savior. He had given them life, for in the seventeenth of John he declares that this is true. They had peace as a possession, for he says, "Peace I leave with you, my peace I give unto you: not as the world giveth, give I unto you. Let not your heart be troubled, neither let it be afraid" (John 14:27). They also had joy as a gift, for he said, "These things have I spoken unto you, that my joy might remain in you, and that your joy might be full" (John 15:11) ; and yet they quarreled among themselves, one of them denied him with an oath, and all of them forsook him.

They were a weak, vacillating company of men, but suddenly there came a remarkable change. It was as if there had been two Peters. The first was a coward, the second a perfect giant in his fearlessness. The first was afraid of a little girl, the second faced a mob and fearlessly proclaimed the truth of God that condemned him; and the secret of this change is found in the fact that the Holy Ghost had fallen upon him and upon them. This is what we need. Jesus was God's gift to the world, and the Holy Ghost is his gift to the Church. Have we failed to take both? A man over in England, telling his pastor about his experience, said that he had taken Jesus for his eternal life and the Holy Ghost for his internal life. This is certainly what we need to do more than anything else. We need the Holy Spirit of God in our lives. He would illuminate our minds as we read the Bible, strengthen our faith as we appropriate Christ, transform our lives as he came to do, and enable us to live and preach in demonstration of the Spirit and with power.

Have you ever stopped to think what is really associated with the full acceptance of the third Person of the Trinity?

First, *Power.* "Ye shall receive power, after that the Holy Ghost is come upon you" (Acts 1:8).

Second, *Ability to pray.* "We know not what we should pray for as we ought: but the Spirit himself itself maketh intercession for us" (Rom. 8:26).

Third, *Victory over sin.* "For the law of the Spirit of life in Christ Jesus hath made me free from the law of sin and death" (Rom. 8:2).

Fourth, *Cleanness of life.* "Ye have purified your souls in obeying the truth through the Spirit" (1 Pet. 1:22).

Fifth, *The representation of Jesus Christ.* Not imitation, but reproduction, is what we need.

Two artists are painting before a picture. The work of one

is sadly deficient, the other an inspiration, for one is copying while the other is reproducing his own work. Oh, that we might be so filled with the Spirit of God that men should take knowledge of us that we not only had been with Jesus but were like him! Two things we need, both of which we may have: *His word and his touch.* First, his Word. We surely have this. Has he not said, "Ye shall receive power"? But with this there is coupled a condition, "Come out from among them, and be ye separate" (2 Cor. 6:17). Fulfilling this condition, we have only to step out upon his promise on the ground of the fact that he had said, "That we might receive the promise of the Spirit through faith" (Gal. 3:14).

Second, we have the touch of his hand. This emphasizes his reality. One of the greatest dangers of the day, it seems to me, is the fact that we are so inclined to make him unreal. It also indicates his nearness. He can fill us so that his life may come throbbing into our very being, and this is the secret of victory in the time of temptation. We must be empty to be filled, but no man can empty himself. Two ways may be presented for the emptying of a jar of air. First, use the air pump; but in this way it cannot be perfectly done. Second, fill the jar with water. This is the better way. When Christ fills our lives he empties us of self and sin. To some unknown friend I am indebted for four steps which we must take if we would be loosed from our bondage and stand straight in the presence of God and men.

First: What God claims I will yield; that is myself.

Second: What I yield God accepts. Since I have taken my hands off from myself I am not my own.

Third: What God accepts he fills.

Fourth: What God fills he uses.

## 34. Do Not Accept Yourself!

G. RAY JORDAN

•

He arose, and came to his father. LUKE 15:20

The exhortation "Accept yourself" has become so popular that millions of people consider it to be one of the wisest insights into life we have ever gained. Many writers insist that ultimately peace of mind is possible only for those who follow these words. In our best moments, however, most of us do not pursue any course blindly, particularly with respect to our own characters.

I. Actually we begin to discover our true selves when we refuse to settle for anything less than the best of which we are capable. Each of us has too many "selves" for us to talk glibly of only one. We well understand what a fictional character of H. G. Wells means by declaring he is not a man, but a mob.

Aristotle pointed out that the most significant facts of life are in the area of possibilities and goals. Thus, our truest nature is in what we can become.

Certainly when most of us observe the contrast between what we are and what we ought to be, we can never be satisfied until we seek the highest that is attainable in life. Indeed, to realize that we have divine potentialities, because we are meant for God, helps us, at least partially, to grasp the significance of being formed "in his image." For, with his aid, we can become increasingly like him.

With respect to this, Thomas à Kempis emphatically declares, "If you seek yourself, you will find yourself and that to your ruin. . . . God does not deceive you; he is deceived who trusts too much to himself." This does not indicate that ours is essentially a Dr. Jekyll-Mr. Hyde problem. Rather, as Anton T. Boisen says, it is one of "a better self, blind and chained and struggling for release."

We do not wonder, therefore, that thousands of visitors to Geneva have been deeply moved as they have gazed above the entrance into the former assembly room of the League of Nations. Looking intently at the figure of a recumbent man who is waking from sleep, they have caught a new vision of life. For, as he reaches for something beyond himself, the man in the artistic creation explains: "Lord of the living and dead, I feel thy finger and find thee." With the same penetrating insight into our possibilities, Wordsworth insists that "there is not a man that lives who has not known his Godlike hours."

Speaking to a young man who had collapsed morally, a pastor declared, "You are a fine, clean, high-minded person." Hearing these words, the youth bowed his head and wept.

The disciples of Christ dramatically demonstrate what all these references mean. We call them *Saint* James, *Saint* John, and *Saint* Peter. Actually they were only ordinary fishermen when Jesus met them. But, as he walked along the shores of the Sea of Galilee, he saw in them "fishers of men"!

II. This New Testament record of "changed lives" explains why Evelyn Underhill writes that our small selves in humble, willed communion with the very Source of our being and power "can grow into tools of the Divine Love and Redeeming Power." Miss Underhill is thinking of the achievement of creative personalities capable of co-operating with the divine action within us.

Lloyd C. Douglas describes what he thinks occurred when Jesus visited Zacchaeus. Jesus, carefully noting the moment of tremendous decision which comes to this tax collector, says to him, "A great salvation has come to your house today." Then Christ asks, "What did you see that made you desire this peace?" Zacchaeus replies, "Good Master, I saw mirrored in your eyes the face of the Zacchaeus I was meant to be."

A soldier of whom Olive Wyon writes discovered this thrilling truth in a most unusual way. When he asked his plastic surgeon to make his face over, the soldier suggested that the physician use as a pattern of procedure the only picture that was hanging on his office wall. This was a portrait of Christ. After the operation was completed and the work of healing was done, the patient made one incisive and unforgettable comment: "If I look so much like him without, I must be more like him within!" This was his resolve. Thus did he give himself to the process of "co-operating" with God in making his character conform to that portrayed by the face of Jesus.

III. This is thrilling—exciting! For in our best moments we seek the Divine Spirit and Godlike power to help us live in the noblest possible way.

With this practical interpretation of redemption in mind, consider an incident of which a friend tells. A Canadian army officer was sneering at a fellow officer for believing in Christianity. "I do not quite see, old man, what your Christ does for you." To this the comrade replied, "Shall I tell you? He can help you be a gentleman in hell." So, as we turn toward—and meditate on—what is good and honest and true and of good report, we can come to our best selves—no matter *where* we are. This is at least part of what "coming home" to God means.

This experience, moreover, causes us to demonstrate the kind of care for people that God himself has for us. Here is genuine Christian evangelism, which is always concerned for the total welfare of all people everywhere.

An act of twenty-five-year-old Reis Leming, an American airman, dramatizes this emphasis. A few years ago, Leming volunteered for rescue work during the disastrous North Sea floods. Using a rubber raft, he waded in water "up to his shoulders" in order to save twenty-seven Britons and Americans in Hunstanton, England. An official referred to this act as "an unbelievable feat of heroism, a magnificent effort, deserving of the highest award." Leming could not swim!

But Leming did show the noblest purpose and spirit of life. So do we, when, by refusing to accept ourselves on any low level, we become our truest selves. Thus do we commit ourselves to Christ and increasingly become like him in attitude, desire, and dedication of ourselves to God's purpose for us.

# V
# THE PERIL
# OF DELAY

## 35. Half-Life

JAMES R. BLACKWOOD

•

Leaving him half dead. LUKE 10:30

This parable of the Jericho road reminds us that if the man who lay in the ditch was a little more than half dead, two of the men who found him there were a little less than half alive.

In the war between life and death, Karl Barth once observed, there are no neutrals, no deserters, no mediators, and no middle ground. You are either dead or alive. Yet one of the most common experiences of the intelligent, now-and-then churchgoer is the sense that he is neither one thing or the other. He believes enough not to be an atheist, but not enough to regard himself as a deeply spiritual man. He is not fully alive; neither is he quite dead. He exists somewhere between in a kind of half-life.

Many, perhaps all of us, feel this way from time to time. Our church is active and alive, or at least far from dead, and yet who can say that it is as dynamic as a church ought to be? At one time or another every member of the church has made public profession of faith in Christ. Today, however, not half our members are here for worship. Obviously we are giving God less than the whole of what we are. Perhaps the wish to bring others to Christ has been the first thing in us to die. In saying this, I speak to myself as well as to you, in order that all of us, together, might see our true condition and so be led to repentance and renewal.

Indeed, the best opportunity for evangelism today is not outside the Church, but inside, revitalizing the faith of those who are already presumed to have it: the half-awake, the half-hearted, the half-convinced, and the half-alive. That is, ourselves.

You and I need the whole Gospel for the whole man. In a popular book for ministers are several scattered references to the resurrection and almost none to the crucifixion. Are we falling back into the pattern of Swinburne's preacher, who "for tender minds served up half a Christ"? Our timid half-life would have it so. But the Gospel itself urges us to say with Paul, "I have been crucified with Christ; it is no longer I who live, but Christ who lives in me" (Gal. 2:20, RSV).

A young and energetic minister felt confident of himself as he began his work in the slums of a Midwestern city. He knew that it was the Christian thing to pick up scraps and leftovers from a glutted industrial society. But his work was not easy. After he had lived with his people a while, he knew more about the Cross than any textbook of theology had ever taught him. He knew the agony of the crucifixion. It took longer for him to know the power of the resurrection. He had not at first believed this in any deep way; it came to him last, as the same truth came to the disciples of Jesus. But what finally came to him took its place at the very center of his belief: the power of resurrection in daily life.

Two men on the Jericho road, a priest and a Levite, were good churchmen, or at least they were not bad churchmen. Yet, in finding the man in the ditch half dead, they needed to know the truth that they were as nearly dead as he.

Surely this parable is for me. Is it for you also? Not because you are an outsider but because you are an insider, the words of Jesus point the way toward repentance and renewal. You are wanted dead or alive, but not halfway between.

If you feel half dead, let the other half die, dying to self in order that you may live to God. "He who loses his life for my sake will find it" (Matt. 10:39, RSV).

Evangelism in the wider sense will begin when you and I move once more in the life and power of the good news we already have.


## 36. Why Are You Not a Christian?

GEORGE W. TRUETT

●

And now, Lord, what wait I for? my hope is in thee. PSALM 39:7

Let me surmise the different things that keep people waiting and away from Christ. Let me give several conjectures, and if I do not give the right conjecture in your case, yet I pray you to face the truth, the principle that shall be discussed, and put to your heart the piercing question: Why am I not a Christian?

I. Do you say, "I am not a Christian because I do not need to be"? The Bible says that every rational being needs God, needs his guidance and forgiveness and help. This Book tells us that no human being has moral resources within himself sufficient to live the life he ought to live, and to meet the destiny out yonder that awaits him. And then we would not fly in the face of Christ, the Light of the world, who came among men and told us all, "You must be born again—every rational human being—you must be born again, born of the Spirit of God, born from above, or you cannot even see the kingdom of God" (see John 3:1-13) . I do not believe, therefore, that a single man or woman would say, "I scout the teaching of the Bible and the teaching of Jesus, and I say I do not need to be a Christian at all."

II. Do you answer, "Sir, I am not one because I cannot believe"? Now, let me ask you, when you say you cannot believe: What is it you cannot believe? Who is it that you cannot believe? There are two pungent questions that all rational men and women must confront. Here they are: "What think ye of Christ?" (Matt. 22:42). That is the first one. And then the other one is: "What shall I do then with Jesus which is called Christ?" (Matt. 27:22). We are every one called to think upon Christ. Who is he? Where did he come from? What did he come for? What did he do for men? What does he propose to do? What can he do? "What think ye of Christ?" And then the other big question—inescapable, inexorable, inevitable question: "What shall I do with Christ?"

Now, we must face those questions. So I ask you, What is there about Christ that troubles you? Here is a great personality that crosses every one of your paths. You must vote for him or vote aagainst him. You must accept him or reject him. You must crown him morally in your heart, or you must morally crucify him. You must be for him or against him. You must be his friend or foe. Now, which ought it to be? Which is sane and reasonable, as you face that inescapable alternative? And I beg you to remember, as you face it, that the wisest and the keenest and the strongest of earth have tried Jesus, and they have found out that he helps. They have found out that he saves. They have found out that he reinforces. And not only the great and strong and intellectual and keen-minded have thus tried Jesus and found him true, but those modest ones who are near and dear to you and me.

III. Do you say, "I am not a Christian because I have too much to give up"? Pray, tell me now, what have you to give up? Jesus, my Savior, and your offered Savior, does not want you to give up anything except that which is wrong, except that which hurts you, except that which poisons you, except that which, if you do not repent of it, shall kill you. Jesus wants you to give up only that which is wrong and blighting and deadly—just that.

IV. Do you say, "I am not a Christian because I am waiting until I get good enough to become one"? Where, pray, will you get your goodness? If you may get your goodness by your own doings, then Jesus need not have come, nor would he have come. Jesus did not come to save good people. He himself tells us, "I am not come to call the righteous, but sinners to repentance" (Matt. 9:13). Thank God! If you are a sinner, you are eligible to be saved.

V. Do you say, "I am waiting until I get strength to live the Christian life"? Then I will pass the question to you and ask you, Where will you get that strength? Jesus not only saves us, but he helps us after he does save us. Paul, that chief apostle, said, "I know whom I have believed, and am persuaded that he is able to keep that which I have committed unto him against that day" (2 Tim. 1:12). Paul did not say that he himself was able to keep himself—never once. Paul said, "By the grace of God I am what I am" (1 Cor. 15:10). He said, "By grace are ye saved through faith; and that not of yourselves: it is the gift of God: not of works, lest any man should boast" (Eph. 2:8-9). Jesus himself says, "You surrender to me and I will forgive and save you. And then I will company with you. I will teach you. I will guide you. I will fortify you. I will empower you. I will strengthen and keep you." That is living the Christian life. Jesus not only starts with us, but he companies with us also as we go on the journey.

## 37. The Waiting Guest

CLOVIS G. CHAPPELL

•

Behold, I stand at the door, and knock: if any man hear my voice, and open the door, I will come in to him, and will sup with him, and he with me. REVELATION 3:20

If Jesus knocks at our doors, how does he knock? He does so in an infinite variety of ways. By every method that divine ingenuity can contrive he seeks an entrance into your heart and mine. Let me name a very few ways in which he knocks at our doors and makes his presence known.

I. He knocks through our failures and through the tragic suffering born of these failures. A man came to see me some time ago who had made a mess of his life, and knew it. Through the days of his young manhood, he had recklessly toyed with an evil habit. He was aware that that habit had enslaved many of his fellows, but he was equally sure that it would never enslave him. But its bonds had tightened little by little until now he knew himself a slave. "The trouble with me," he said, "is that I have no inner reserves. As long as I talk to you I will stand, but I know that as soon as this conversation is over, I'll turn back to my old slavery." God was knocking at his door through a sense of his own wretchedness and helplessness.

I met another man who felt no sense of slavery at all, but life had grown as stale upon his lips as bread made of ashes. He saw no meaning in life. Once he had dreamed of being and doing something worth while. But something happened. He felt that a Christian friend had let him down; so his zest had gone. He was bored, fed up, greeting the fresh opportunities of each morning, not with enthusiastic joy, but with sleepy yawns. Christ was knocking at his door through his boredom.

II. Christ knocks at our door through the vision of our better selves. One day as he stood on the banks of the river Jordan, he saw a blundering fisherman coming his way. As he looked at him, he saw not only the man that he was but the man that he was capable of becoming. "Thou art Simon the son of Jona," he said with enthusiasm: "thou shalt be called Cephas, which is by interpretation, A stone" (John 1:42). Simon never forgot that word. Always he must have seen out ahead of him the gallant-hearted, Christlike man in whom Jesus had made him believe. When cowardice had make him afraid even to acknowledge the master that he loved, when he had fallen into utter shame, he could not despair. He went out and wept bitterly, hating himself for the thing he was, but still tormented by the possibilities of the man that he might become. So Christ is knocking at your door.

III. Christ knocks through our sense of inadequacy. He disturbs us by the realization that comes to us sooner or later if we are really earnest people that in our own strength we cannot realize our better selves. From generation to generation, through all the centuries, every man seems to have to learn for himself of his inability to save himself. We look at our Lord and see in him how life ought to be lived. We see in him the vision of our possibilities. But when we set out to attain, if we struggle in our own strength alone, we meet little other than persistent defeat. Christ knocks at our hearts not only through our inadequacy, our inability to *become* our best, but also through our inability to *do* our best.

IV. Finally, he is knocking through every precious memory of our better yesterdays. He is knocking through the voice of his Word when we give it a chance to speak to us. He is knocking even through the appeal of the minister. In a thousand ways, by every means that infinite ingenuity can contrive, the Christ of God is seeking to enter into your life. He is seeking to make it possible for you to experience with Paul "the glory of this mystery . . . which is Christ in you" (Col. 1:27). He is seeking to enable you to shout with this great apostle, "I am crucified with Christ: nevertheless I live; yet not I, but Christ liveth in me" (Gal. 2:20). You may have the Risen Christ for your very own guest if you will.

## 38. On Your Terms or His?

DONALD MACLEOD

•

"Lord, I will follow thee; but. . . ." LUKE 9:61

There are three totalitarian powers at work in the world today and they are seeking to lay claim upon any human soul who stands ready. One originates in Moscow; another, totalitarian secularism, is rampant in our Western civilization; and the third comes down from heaven. These three, moreover, are somewhat causally related. For if you reject the third, the one that comes down from heaven, you fall victim inevitably to the second, the one that is active in our own environment. And if you persist in entertaining and cherishing the second, you will be fair game for the cool strategy of the first.

The third totalitarian power, we said, came down from heaven and may be called the totalitarian God, who by his very nature lays a constant claim upon his creatures. Throughout the Old Testament we sense his yearning pursuit in the frequently recurring phrase, "My people." In the New Testament, this same God becomes man in Jesus Christ and gives his matchless and unsullied life as an offering on Calvary in order to redeem men and make them his own. And onward through the life of the Church, this desire for all nations has spearheaded every evangelical effort to call men to own him as King and Lord. This God is totalitarian, but in a completely different sense from the others. True, he demands all we are and have, but he will never press his demand through force. He confronts us in all the awesomeness of his Being, but his method is the constraint of redemptive love. Never does he impose himself upon us. He demands only free loyalty. "Behold, I stand at the door, and knock: if any man hear my voice, and open the door, I will come in" (Rcv. 3:20). It is we who must be willing to open the door. And thereby God does not produce a type, nor does he pour your personality into a mold and circumscribe or stunt your independent aspirations. Each individual, you and I and the man down the street, has his place in God's great family where his powers are free to develop, grow, and lift.

Now what is so baffling and strange to us is that this third totalitarian powcr, though endorsed by the testimony of history and the witness of generations of redeemed lives, claims a smaller number of persons actually than the other two named. Why? The reason is that most people fail to see that the ultimate significance and value of life is realized only insofar as one does with life what God wants and demands. And God calls for absolute moral obedience and unconditional spiritual surrender. Our devotion to this Eternal God has been sporadic, anemic, and cold. We have been so busy with ourselves and so fully engaged in running from this fear and that, that our response to his claim has been like the man whom Jesus called and who answered, "Lord, I will follow thee; but . . . ."

Look at the picture this text presents. Jesus was coming, as it were, to the very cdgc of destiny. He had set his face as a flint to go to Jerusalem to answer with his life the claim his Father had laid upon his spirit. On the way thrcc men appeared who look in the direction of the kingdom, but who refuse to go all out for any cause on account of certain reservations within themselves. Their attitudes may be summed up in the text, "Lord, I will follow thee; but . . . ."

I. The first one meets Jesus, and with a flourish of enthusiasm says, "Lord, I will follow thee whithersoever thou goest." Jesus' immediate reaction was, in a sense, "Come, by all means, come! but remember, 'Foxes have holes, and the birds of the air have nests; but the Son of man hath not where to lay his head.' "

Is he one of us? How many of us have volunteered under the banner of Jesus without stopping long enough to investigate the price? John R. Mott said, "Christ never hid his scars to win a disciple." To all those who would accept too readily the claim of a totalitarian God, Jesus flings out the challenge of the cost. Have you or I said, "Lord, I will follow thee," but when he showed us what it involved we drew back and protested, "But, oh! the cost"?

II. The second man whom Jesus called replied, "Suffer me first to go and bury my father." This was a clear case of what H. D. A. Major once called "a conflict of loyalties." This man had not realized that he was up against the most critical and urgent matter of all human experience. "Let the dead bury their dead," said Jesus. This was the job of those who were still unaware of "the great new fact" of their time. The kingdom demanded action then or not at all. Possibly, we too are willing to enlist, but not yet. "Go away, Master, I'm busy with other matters just now. Come back when I shall have more time."

III. The third man who volunteers hastened to add a condition. He wanted an interim holiday in order to have a round of farewells among his folk and possibly to make his new venture more auspicious. Jesus, however, wrote him off with a stroke of finality, "No man, having put his hand to the plough, and looking back, is fit for the kingdom of God."

Unfortunately, so many find themselves ready to enlist but always on their own terms. Imagine any one of our great missionaries saying, "I'll do everything I can for India, Africa, or South America, provided I can do it at home." There are scores among the rank and file of everyday church members whose greater usefulness for the kingdom of God is utterly frustrated because their service is dependent upon, and measured by, their own terms.

Christ today claims you and me to work for him, to live for

him, and if need be to die for him. To offer him merely a fraction of our devotion is to let him down. To give him a place off-center in our life is to insult him. In his program, real faith is a passion, an enthusiasm, and a consuming zeal that eats up all our life and sends us out upon errands which the world calls mad. The issue therefore is clear: either the glittering toys of the first two totalitarian powers now and the bitter price later, or the claim of Christ with the cost today and the glory tomorrow. Thousands of born-again Christians urge us to decide one hundred per cent for him. It will not be so difficult if we can pray the words of Reginald Heber's stirring hymn:

> They climbed the steep ascent of heaven
> Through peril, toil, and pain.
> O God to us may grace be given
> To follow in their train.

# 39. Life's Criminal Agnosticism

## William A. Quayle

•

And knew not that it was Jesus. JOHN 20:14

Mary was in the garden. Some of us miss the sight of Christ because we are looking at the garden. Is it possible for one beauty, very winsome, to drown another beauty more winsome? Yes; quite possible. Is God's garden fair? So fair. Is it meant for us to be in? Meant for all of us to be in. Know you why God made so many flowers? Answer—So everybody could have a choice. Know you why God made so many trees? So everybody could have a shadow. Know you why God made so many rivulets? So everybody might have a song. Know you why God made so many waves? So everybody might rock upon a billow. Know you why God made so many sunsets? So that everyone could pluck a crimson rose that vanishes with the daylight, and wear it at the heart. So beautiful, thank God, this out-of-doors—this garden of our God.

And it were a pity then if when the perfume of the garden is so sweet and when the crimson of the flower is so seashell delicate, and when the odor from the dank woods drenches not the body but the spirit, a pity that in the presence of the garden and with the mantle of the garden, so to say, wrapped around the shoulders, we should miss the Gardener. Ah, that is it. I have known many dwellers in the outdoors to miss the Gardener. I have known many a lover of the sky to miss the Sky-maker. I have known many a lover of bulbs to miss the marvel of him who put the germ within the bulbs. The garden is so fair. Because I saw the cloud should I let the cloud so swathe me round about as that I missed him who dropped the cloud for a shadow to the panting flocks and the lowing herds and the weary child and the burdened man? Should I? No. We must not let the garden keep us from the Gardener. We must not let the thing keep us from the Contriver. This is the divine gift then of scenting out the path that leads to the hand, and following the hand through the arm to the shoulder, and running the shoulder home to the heart. O, heart, that is the trouble. We didn't know that the fingers run to the palm and the palm to the wrist and the wrist to the elbow and the elbow to the shoulder, all slanting upward, and then that the shoulder runs, slanting downward to the heart; else hand and fingers and pulse and power be dead. It is the heart that giveth life.

What is the garden? Why, it is one method of the Gardener's talking. What is the flower? It is the thing God loves to look at. What is the star? It is a touch of the finger of God in the canopy of night. And where God's finger touches he leaves light. Ah, heart, who is around? Why, the Gardener is around. But you ought to know that the Gardener is not anonymous. Who is around? The Gardener. And I didn't see him!

Do you read John Burroughs? He missed the Gardener. Burroughs was apparently an agnostic. I have gone through all of his books, seen him walk on his dirt, gone down among the water lilies with him, stopped on the Hudson banks with him, heard the water brooks bubbling strangely intelligible speech with him, have been all wheres with him, but never saw a hint about the Gardener. And I am so sorry about it. If he only once had looked in the Gardener's face and said, "I bless thee, Gardener, that the garden is so sweet," Burroughs would have had no superior in the earth as an interpreter of the out-of-doors. But in the garden he missed the Gardener. We must not, must we now? We must not miss the Gardener. Is he not at home? I call you to mark that you are out in God's flower garden, all a-bloom and all a-perfume, and all a-rapture of green. Don't miss the Gardener and say, "He is not at home." And some of us, therefore, are guilty of criminal agnosticism in that we miss the Gardener because we watch the garden.

## 40.  The Man Who Stood in a Basket

WILLIAM GODDARD SHERMAN

•

I am the way, and the truth, and the life; no one comes to the Father, but by me. JOHN 14:6, RSV

In a little thatch-roofed church in Africa a commitment service was being conducted by a missionary. The faithful converts to Christ brought their gifts—fruits, vegetables, poultry, whatever they possessed—to dedicate to the Lord's work. One by one they made their way to the front of the little church and gave their offering. But one young African was too poor to bring an offering. For a long time he stood in deep sadness at the rear of the church. He loved the Lord and wanted to present a gift. The tears welled up in his eyes as he saw others placing their tokens of love in the baskets, for he had nothing to give. Then suddenly he knew what he would do, and he made an offering which overshadowed every other gift. Going forward, he stepped into the basket and with hands folded, head bowed, and eyes closed in prayer, he remained there. He was giving himself to Christ.

The key word at the heart of the Christian Gospel is love. The love of God brought the world into being; it brought life and immortality to light; it brought the soul's salvation to reality. This Divine Love has been extended to us, calling us to drink at the fountain of everlasting life. We too must "stand in the basket" and commit ourselves unreservedly to this saving grace.

We live in a world which, seemingly, ever increases in complexities and anxieties. Yet the Gospel of Christ remains as simple as it ever was, and God's desire is still that whosoever will may come to drink at this unfailing fountain. He has filled his universe with his majesty and, if we desire, our souls with his Spirit. God is present everywhere and in countless ways. Someone has said, "Thou dost surround, envelop, and penetrate us." Despite the confusion and complexity of our modern world, to find God is still a simple matter. For God is searching for us! The tremendous truth which is vital for every man is that if we want God, we may have him. All we need do is respond to his love and receive Christ's salvation on faith.

The tragedy of our age is that we abandon the One—the only One—who can save us. In a great city at 2 A.M. the phone rang in the home of a noted surgeon. The surgeon was told that a young man lay near death following an automobile accident. The patient was in a small hospital twenty miles from the city, and the great surgeon was the only man within calling distance who could possibly save his life. Hurriedly, the doctor dressed. As he drove in haste toward the nearby town, he stopped for a traffic light. At that moment someone opened his car door and put a gun to his ribs. "Just drive," he ordered.

All efforts on the part of the surgeon to explain his mission were fruitless. When they came to the town the man with the gun ordered the surgeon to stop. Again the doctor tried to explain, but the man ordered him out of the car. Helplessly, the surgeon watched as a man in a brown coat and gray trousers, and a cap pulled over his eyes, drove away in his automobile. By the time the doctor reached the hospital he was told that he had arrived too late. The young man had only moments before died. One of the nurses said, "The boy's father is here and needs comforting. Will you speak to him?"

The doctor walked into the waiting room and found the sobbing father. He was wearing a brown coat and gray trousers, and by his side was a cap. He was the man who had taken the car. Surely this true story is a parable of life. So frequently we force from our lives the very one who could save us.

Have you trusted in Jesus Christ for saving and redeeming love? Have you stood in the basket and committed yourself and all that you have to him who redeemed your soul by his death on the Cross?

## 41. What Do You Most Want?

PAUL P. FRYHLING

•

If you were asked what you want most in life, your immediate answer might be, Things, enjoyable activity, and success. These are, of course, not bad in themselves, but are they really what you most covet?

A small boy is a bundle of activity. His day is filled with little things that are important to him. He achieves great success as his fertile imagination moves from "general" to "explorer" or "space expert" or even "president." He does not need mother and may indeed resent her occasional intrusions when she calls him to lunch or checks on his wearing apparel. But when his energy is spent, he forgets his proud conquests and seeks shelter and rest in mother's care. He really most wants to be at home in the family.

We too want and need something more than things, activity, and success. In any final analysis, we want to be confident in a relationship to God. We want to feel and know that we are accepted and secure as a child of God in God's family.

Why does everyone not have this quiet confidence? A youth who has done something wrong is afraid of what his father will say. So he runs away. Then someone tells him that his father will forgive him and welcome him home. But the boy decides he is not worthy and must suffer by himself for his wrong. In reality, he is refusing to believe that his father loves him.

Even so, you may be running from God because some things in your life are wrong. Many people have heard that God will forgive and welcome them back, but they refuse the invitation which Jesus Christ offers, or at least they have never taken definite action on it. "He came unto his own, and his own received him not" (John 1:11).

If this is your situation, and you want more than anything else to be right with God, here are three steps by which to become a child of God.

I. *Admit.* The two things you must admit are your desire and your depravity. Your desire must be a sincere and earnest longing to have above everything else peace with God in your heart. When you really desire to be right with God, you have taken the important first step. Your depravity calls for an honest and sober admission of sinfulness and separation from God. Not only do you confess to having committed sin, but also that you have an inner sinfulness, a tendency to wrong, in your very nature. You have deliberately refused to let God have his way in your life. You are a sinful person.

II. *Accept.* The second step is to accept. This is where the change takes place. Look carefully at this clear word from the Gospel of John, "But to all who received him, who believed in his name, he gave power to become children of God" (John 1:12, RSV). The two things you must do are to receive and to believe. First, receive Jesus Christ. When a friend comes to your door, you simply open the door and say, "Come in." You do not have to search for your friend; he is at the door and wishes to enter. You receive your friend by opening the door and admitting him.

Jesus says, "Behold, I stand at the door and knock; if any one hears my voice and opens the door, I will come in" (Rev. 3:20, RSV). So you may pray, "Lord, I want you in my heart and life. Come in!" He will. This means that you "receive him."

Second, believe in his Name. The name "Jesus" literally means "Savior." To believe in his Name then means truly to believe that Jesus Christ is the Son of God sent from heaven, who died on the Cross and rose again for the sins of the world, and also to trust him as your personal Savior, accepting the forgiveness and cleansing of your sins made possible through his atoning blood.

So you may pray, "Lord, to the best of my ability, I now believe that you died for me, and I accept the salvation you offer to all who receive and believe in you." This is "believing in his name" unto salvation.

When you have done this, the Word says that God gives the power to become a child of God. An action from God takes place as the Holy Spirit makes you spiritually new.

III. *Acknowledge.* Now that you have admitted your need and accepted God's remedy for it, acknowledge what God has done. Thank the Lord and give testimony of your confidence that his provision and promise are true. Not to acknowledge would mean that you question God's truthfulness or his ability.

Acknowledge the *gift of God.* "By grace you have been saved through faith; and this is not your own doing, it is the gift of God—not because of works, lest any man should boast" (Eph. 2:8-9, RSV). You are a child of God by his gift, not by your efforts or worthiness.

Acknowledge the *power of God.* John speaks of the children

of God as those "who were born, not of blood [not by inheritance or family relationship] nor of the will of the flesh [not by
personal effort or will] nor of the will of man [not by human
organization], but of God" (John 1:13, RSV). Your works could
not accomplish this, however determined your effort. God alone
has the power to do it.

Acknowledge the *love of God*. You know God can make you
his child, but why should he do this? There is only one answer:
God's love. "God so loved the world that he gave" (John 3:16).
"See what love the Father has given us, that we should be called
children of God; and so we are" (1 John 3:1, RSV).

Acknowledge the *Word of God*. His promise of salvation and
the record of his action to provide it are in his Word, the Bible.
Trust what the Bible says; rely upon God's Word without
doubt.

Take these three steps: admit your sinful need, accept what
Jesus has done for you, and acknowledge that you have received
God's gift of salvation. This is the way to gain that which you
want above all else—to become a child of God.

## 42. The Slavery of Sin

### RICHARD CHENEVIX TRENCH

•

Whosoever committeth sin is the servant of sin. JOHN 8:34

We hear these words, and they do not reveal to us the consequences of sin under a new and terrible aspect. This they will
only do when we give to the word "servant," or "slave" as it
might be rendered, the emphasis which the Divine Speaker
meant that it should have. "He that committeth sin is the *slave
of sin*." That Lord who in so many gracious ways has sought to
scare and separate us from evil, does so here by setting forth to

us that it is a slavery; that however men may think and fancy at the beginning that their sins shall be servants to them it is never long before they inevitably become the servants to their sins.

He would teach us this, and all experience confirms it, that any willful sin, admitted into the heart, having once gained a footing there, cannot remain at a standstill, but must ever bring more and more the whole man under its dominion, laying ever new and ever stronger fetters upon him; so that the chains of evil habits which may have been but as spider threads at the first, so easily might they by a vigorous effort of the will have been snapped asunder, become links of iron at the last.

He would bid us know that sin, this tyrannous mistress of our lives, puts him who has accepted her yoke ever to viler drudgeries. Many things which he would have shrunk back from at first, while his conscience was yet unseared, he being past feeling does greedily at the last, and without hesitation or remorse: small sins in him growing into great, the petty purloiner from the common stock into the traitor who sold his Lord; sins of desire turning into sins of act; the cockatrice's egg hatching into the fiery flying serpent; the man falling from one wickedness to another; and because he did not like to retain God in his knowledge, being given over to vile affections and to those penal blindnesses with which, by an inexorable law, God visits and avenges the free indulgence in unlawful desires.

*Why* it is that sin has this fearful power of enslaving those who had no intention of yielding themselves absolutely and without reserve to its dominion—of growing, increasing, more and more leavening the whole life, penetrating it through and through, till, it may be, the whole is leavened; how it comes to pass that no man can say, "Thus far I will advance in sin and no further," or "In this I will allow myself, but then I will stop short"—why it is that all such calculations are sure to be defeated, and that none can measure out to himself the exact amount of evil which he will commit? The reason is that no sin, however separable or separate from other sins it may seem, can be regarded as an isolated thing; every sin stands in connection with a whole spiritual kingdom of darkness, from which it came forth and with which it maintains correspondencies and relations still, even after it has found lodgment in the sinner's heart.

The existence of this dark kingdom, this kingdom of envy and hate and lust and pride, which is around us, and would fain be within us—the existence of Satan and his angels, of these tempters ever watchful to find an open door in the heart, and where that door has been opened but for one sin, by force or fraud to make an entrance for many—this fact that there is a kingdom of darkness around us, as well as a kingdom of light, that we have affinities with the one no less than with the other, and that sins no less than graces are linked together by a mysterious law one with another, it is this which explains to us the deep significance of the Psalmist's prayer, "Keep back thy servant also from presumptuous sins; let them not have dominion over me" (Ps. 19:13). It is this which forbids us to believe that any sin, willfully admitted into a heart, will remain quiescent there; which makes us sure that it must stir and move, must cast forth its roots and fibers on every side, must gradually vitiate and corrupt portions hitherto sounder and sincerer of the life no less than that part which it originally claimed for its own. Nay, not merely *some* portions, but *all*—perhaps itself gradually taking possession of all. For oftentimes a ruling sin will have power little by little to color the whole life with its own tints; to assimilate everything there to itself—as in ever wider circles to absorb all into its own vortex, being as it were a gulf, a maelstrom, into which all which was better and nobler in the man is irresistibly attracted and drawn, and is there swallowed up, and forever disappears.

# VI
# WORDS OF
# ETERNAL LIFE

# 43. To Whom Shall We Go?

### W. A. CAMERON

•

Simon Peter answered him, Lord, to whom shall we go? thou hast the words of eternal life. JOHN 6:68

When we turn to Christ we find, like Peter, that he has *the words of eternal life*. For one thing, he had brought a new conception of life itself. That word "life" contains the master enigma of our existence. A recent book on medical psychology contains this statement: "The great difficulty is that we do not know what life really is. But we may hope that science will soon solve that problem." Life brings science itself face to face with mystery. At the top of the ladder of life is man. Compared with all other forms of life, how majestic he seems. He stands at the top of creation. And yet the shadow of impermanence lies over him and all his works. Nothing lasts. The individual vanishes after a few years and civilizations after a few centuries. However great life is it is incomplete. It hints at something beyond. It stirs within us a desire for life that is life indeed. Such a life has been raised above the conditions of time. "This is life eternal . . . [to] know thee the only true God, and Jesus Christ, whom thou hast sent" (John 17:3). If Jesus Christ is life eternal then I may invite the life eternal in. I may ask him to dwell in me and be my life. All who have genuinely experienced this will find it easy to feel the deep significance of life.

Jesus brought a new conception of what makes life worth while. The world has its own idea of blessedness or success and has expressed it in various forms. We can find it everywhere. What do men say? "Blessed is the man who is always right, who is always satisfied with himself; blessed is the man who is strong and who rules, the man who is rich and popular and enjoys life." These are the obvious things by which to weigh success. Their possession makes men happy; their loss makes men sad. Now it may come as a shock when we notice that not one of these things entered the mind of Jesus when he treated of the things that make life worth living. Blessed, said he, is the man who thinks lowly of himself, who has passed through great trials, who longs for perfection, who carries a tender heart, who has a passion for holiness, who sweetens human life and dares to be true to conscience.

Jesus once told the story of a farmer whose barns bulged but whose soul shrank. One day this farmer patted himself on the back and said, Now you have great wealth in store for years to come, so take it easy; eat, drink, and enjoy yourself. But that very night he died. Jesus said that he was a fool. And Jesus is right. He carries the moral consent of mankind. These things are so. They do come first. There is nothing else that matters. And we can see it, now that Jesus has said it. We certainly agree with Peter that he had the words of eternal life.

These are but two of many ways in which we can try to tell what Jesus means for the world and for ourselves. It is only when you and I take this life of Jesus and set it to the music of our faith and penitence and endeavor, that we really grasp the meaning of it. He knew the way to God. He lived life right out and tried its issues right through. He shrank neither from life's pain, nor from its tragedy, but he never doubted its nobility. He revealed Divine Love by his suffering and opened heaven by his Cross. Whatever he touched he transformed. Jesus lived life in its wholeness. He essayed the heights. He did not shrink from the depths. Three years he lived before men, yet, as Dr. Orchard once put it, "In that time he managed to let eternity break through, and lifted man's horizons to infinity. He took all that came to him and turned it to the purpose of his mission: circumstance, failure, disappointment, and death. They gave him a manger for a cradle, a bench for a pulpit, thorns for a crown, and a cross for a throne; but he took them and made them the very glory of his career. He turned sorrow into joy. He found strength in labor, peace in the storm, rest on the Cross, and life in the grave." If we really believe this we shall put him at the center of our lives. We shall put him at the center of our social relationships. We shall refuse every way of life but his, and say with Peter, "Lord, to whom shall we go? thou hast the words of eternal life. And we believe and are sure that thou art that Christ, the Son of the living God."

## 44. The Word of God

J. WALLACE HAMILTON

•

God, who at sundry times and in divers manners spake in time past unto the fathers by the prophets, hath in these last days spoken unto us by his Son. HEBREWS 1:1-2

The ultimate Word is the living Word, the Word in Christ made flesh, God speaking his mind through the living expression of a Person. Christmas did not come to an unprepared world. When the fullness of time had come, when the rightness of time arrived, God sent forth his Son. Many were the fore-gleams of his coming. Many were the little lamps along the road to Bethlehem. For hundreds of years the Greeks had been talking about the Word, "the emanation," "the universal reason," "the active presence of the god." And for longer years the Jews had held the promise of a Child born, a Son given whose name would be called Wonderful, Emmanuel, the God in our midst who would save his people from their sins.

I suppose you could go through the Old Testament and trace out almost all of the things Jesus said, in some form, in little fragments and partial glimpses. But the thesis of the New Testament is that neither the Gentile philosopher who bowed before the gods of nature, nor the religious Jew who possessed the righteous law, had learned the meaning of the great Word. At best they were little lamps, little signals pointing in the darkness. The insights of the past are not to be despised. The moral gropings in the darkness are not to be despised. The little lights along the road are not to be despised. But when the great sun comes up and daylight dawns, we no longer need to light the little lamps. In him was life, and that life was the light of men.

If you want to hear the clearest Word of God, you will not find it out there in nature's book, in mathematics, music, science, or beauty; nor in the abstract words of Plato, in philosophy; nor in the burning words of Moses and the prophets. "This is my beloved Son . . . ," said the Voice from the cloud, "hear ye him" (Matt. 17:5). Why don't we? Here is the mind and heart and nature of the living God, brought near, spelled out in the language of a life. There has never been anything like him on this earth. Nineteen centuries have been looking at that life with microscopic scrutiny and have yet to find one flaw, one moral failure, one unworthy thought. The perfect revelation has been made.

Some complain that they cannot understand the Incarnation. Well, I hope they can't! It would be too small a fact if we could get our minds around it. But I also hope that it means more to you than literature, more than reading matter in a book. Those who wrote about it were not copying out of any book; they were writing out of their experience of a personal discovery they had made. Paul for example! Paul had struggled up through all the human ways of trying to find God. He had been trained in the knowledge of the law. He had a powerful mind that could wrap itself around the most profound philosophy of the ancients. But one day on the road to Damascus he made a personal discovery. Out on that lonely road it came home to him that God was in Christ reconciling the world to himself. And from there on, all he cared to talk about was the knowledge of God that comes through Jesus Christ. And the more deeply he thought into the mystery of the Incarnation, the more he believed that the world's most desperate need was to know this Word of God, the living Word, the Word which in Christ had come alive to walk our dusty human roads.


## 45.  The Centrality of the Resurrection

Bryant M. Kirkland

•

He is not here: for he is risen, as he said. Come, see the place where the Lord lay. Matthew 28:6

Christianity is more than a Christmas religion; it is an Easter faith. From the human side, more people probably think of it as a Yuletide story of peace and goodwill; but from the viewpoint of the New Testament, the preponderance of emphasis and evidence makes Christianity a resurrection faith.

I. The resurrection of Jesus Christ is central to an understanding of evangelical Christianity because it validates the promises and claims of the Lord to be the unique Savior of modern men and women. The resurrection is a singular event because it furnishes the attestation which makes him a significant person for people of our time who have neither seen him nor have any other way of validating their belief.

The importance of the doctrine of the resurrection needs to be better understood in its relationship to the whole system of Christian belief and action. Jesus made it central to his teachings. When his antagonists pressed him near the end of his life, he said, "And I, if I be lifted up from the earth, will draw all men unto me" (John 12:32). And St. Paul emphasized the Easter message in his preaching when he said, "If Christ be not raised, your faith is vain; ye are yet in your sins" (1 Cor. 15:17). In other words, "If our preaching has no resurrection value in it, then is our faith dead, and we are yet in our sins."

II. The cold movement of rationalism has tried to overcome the resurrection problem in Christianity by evasion, denial, and more customarily by subjectivizing or spiritualizing it. When Adolf Harnack began his liberalization of Christian teachings, his old father, Theodosius Harnack, wrote to him, "Where you stand with regard to the fact of the resurrection is in my eyes no longer Christian theology. To me Christianity stands or falls with the resurrection."

This same spirit of questioning and affirming the resurrection which was characteristic of the past is also indicative of the present religious situation. Many men and women find it difficult to believe in the resurrection of Christ or to form an adequate concept of its meaning. But when they do believe in it and frame a doctrine of its meaning, then they find an energizing force behind their faith and a motivating spirit behind their conduct.

When St. Paul addressed the distinguished Greeks in Athens, we find not only that he came to grips with the central fact of the resurrection, but also that the listeners scorned it even as much as the modern world does. They responded readily when he proclaimed merely a God of nature and creation. But when he avowed that he preached Jesus Christ risen from the dead, some of them slapped their thighs in mirth and scorned, saying that it is impossible (see Acts 17:22-32).

III. The resurrection faith is the central doctrine of the Christian Gospel. The conflict of this issue is of great significance to the transforming message of personal hope, to the energy of effective Christian ethics, and to the divine psychiatry of individually changed lives.

We are reduced to the alternatives about the resurrection that either it is a factual event of objective and subjective meaning or, if there is no reality to the empty tomb and risen Lord, we are the victims of a continuing illusion and the unknowing perpetuators of a great ruse. Hardheaded thinking would then lead us to the conclusion first preached at Corinth: we have an empty tomb and no rationale to account for it. We have a good man whom everyone calls the best person and yet wittingly or not he exaggerated his claims or else we misunderstood him.

So the Easter faith becomes crucial to the angle with which the Church approaches the world with its radical good news, or else merges into the syncretistic stream of human wistfulness echoed in the words, "We trusted that it had been he which should have redeemed Israel: and beside all this, today is the third day since these things were done" (Luke 24:21).

Modern disciples can still validate the resurrection faith on the Emmaus road of inquiry. The fact of the empty tomb, the transformation of the unbelieving disciples, the spread of the Christian Church, the vitalization of individuals throughout history, and the witness of the Spirit within the heart's experience all attest, "He is risen, as he said."

## 46. The Weight Is on Him

CHARLES T. SARDESON

•

Atonement is God's idea and the stewardship of his own love. It is a victory won by the Son of God over all the powers of this world, over all the wrongness in the lives of men. Through his death and by his resurrection Christ frees life from the fatal grip of any adversary and insures its future. The whole cry of the New Testament is the glad news of atonement, and all the credit is ascribed to the Lord upon the throne of grace. The atonement is God's event.

Of all the great words in our vocabulary, this stands foremost. It gives substance to the rest and passes judgment on every inadequate idea. It cuts the ground out from under those who would find God in nature or in any human effort. Atonement forms a dead end to the hopes of those who bank on any inevitable success of social progress or to those who believe in the ultimate winning out of human effort to the high reaches of heaven. Atonement places the strength and witness of a Christian life solidly where they belong, in the life and spirit of the Gospel, in the fact of Jesus the Christ.

Our finest thinking becomes dull brass before this truth. That all the holiness of heaven should come knocking on the door of any life for admittance is bewildering in itself; but beyond that, to realize that he must bear the shame of what he finds in us to win us back is overwhelming indeed.

The longing to atone is God's eternal attitude. It is more than a single page in history, the event of one chapter. On that dark hill when his heart ached with such vast hurt that even the nails must have seemed welcome release, he was declaring himself and his intentions toward his people for all time.

Only against a background like that can you see the real tragedy of our time. It is not fundamentally a tragedy of human failures and great weariness and crumbling hopes. It is the boundless love of God beaten and bruised and whipped that forms the real tragedy. It is the sight of that awful love bearing the shame that flows from the wrongness in our lives. Atonement is the patient endurance of the Eternal in the meanest depths to which life could drag him, placing in that very spot a cross and a wild, clear hope.

With all this, however, the outline of the word is still not firmly marked without one more fact. When God breaks down the barriers between himself and us, when he enters into a man's life to heal and lift it unto himself, he also shatters the barriers between man and his fellow men. Here stands the hope of the world—that in the magnificent, atoning love of God we may know one another. Until that moment we are a world of strangers forever at odds with ourselves and wholly unable to know and love our neighbor.

Wherever you may start in your thinking about the ultimate destiny of your own life, you can be certain that you will be compelled to get hold of this word before you can make any adequate beginning at all, before you can get a stone's throw along the way. For it is here that God makes his beginning with life. He never begins by handling the stuff of which you are made, never with any scrutiny of your fitness. God begins by confronting you with the quality of his own life, with the full measure of his own love. He does it precisely to show what your life is by itself and how he takes the shame of what it is after you've seen it—atonement never comes cheaply—and carries it off himself. Then in the place of your shame he leaves freedom, understanding, and such a heart of praise that it sounds for all the world like the full peal of many bells or the strong confession of a great soul.

## 47. The Light That Shines Forever

CARL F. H. HENRY

•

And the light shineth in darkness; and the darkness comprehended it not. JOHN 1:5

The contrast of light and darkness is a familiar Biblical motif. In Genesis it appears in the created sequence of night and day; elsewhere in the Pentateuch, in the cloud by day and pillar of fire by night; in the prophetic writings, in the light to arise and shine upon the Gentiles. The motif remains throughout the Gospels, in the Book of Acts, in the Epistles, and even into the Book of Revelation. One can, in fact, summarize the story of creation, of revelation, of regeneration, of sanctification, and of final glorification in these words: "And God said, Let there be light: and there was light" (Gen. 1:3).

This motif appears in one of the most familiar yet elusive passages in the Bible, the prologue of John's Gospel: "And the light shineth in darkness; and the darkness comprehended it not." Two elements of special interest in this verse are, first, the tense of the Greek verb *phainō* in the first clause and, second, the meaning of *katalambanō*, the Greek verb in the closing clause.

The light, John writes, *shines* in the darkness. The Greek tense is present. The light *is shining* in the darkness, or, as in *The New English Bible*, "The light shines on in the dark." The shining light is the Logos, the Divine Agent in creation and in redemption. As the eternal Christ once lighted the primal creation when it was a desolation and waste—"without form, and void" (Gen. 1:2)—so too he illumines the darkness of the fallen world of sin and shame. He did not say simply "I was," but rather "I *am* the light of the world" (John 8:12). The light shines even here and now.

The translators seem to tumble over each other in their rendering of the verb *katalambanō*. The Authorized Version reads "and the darkness comprehended it not," that is, failed to grasp the light and remains in darkness still. The Revised Standard Version, on the other hand, reads "and the darkness has not overcome it," meaning, to put it out. *The New English Bible* suggests in the words "the darkness has never quenched it" that the light is inextinguishable. The Greek word *katalambanō* bears a variety of meanings, among them, to perceive, apprehend, and overtake. Is the Apostle John simply telling us that the darkness has not perceived the light or that the light keeps shining despite every effort of darkness to quench it? Is John commenting on the character of the darkness or is he making an affirmation about the light? Does he merely affirm the depth of iniquity or declare also the inextinguishability of the light?

We must do as the translators have done when they are unsure of the precise meaning of a word. That is, to search the context for a clue.

I. Much in the context supports the emphasis that the darkness is stubborn toward, and uncomprehending of, the light. Recall these important ingredients of John's Gospel: "He came unto his own, and his own [his own creation, his own people] received him not" (1:11). In their unbelief, even his brethren repeatedly urge him to go to Jerusalem and manifest himself openly (see 7:3-9). Jesus is betrayed and scourged, and the Jews cry out, "Away with him, away with him, crucify him" (19:15). In a biting comment to Nicodemus, the Savior says, "This is the condemnation, that light is come into the world, and men loved darkness rather than light" (3:19). "The light shineth in darkness; and the darkness comprehended it not."

We need to hear afresh the emphasis of the text. Modern man minimizes the depth of this darkness. By calling the darkness light, he attempts to dispense with the need for supernatural light. When John writes of darkness, he exempts no generation of fallen history. Darkness is John's word for the ambiguous enterprise that we so often dignify by such terms as human culture and civilization of which we are often tempted to speak only good. Darkness is his word for the whole gamut of human life insofar as it is without God and without grace.

II. But is this the emphasis which John really has most in mind? Does he think of the dread reality of darkness or does he pass beyond the fact of darkness to say something about the persistence and inextinguishability of the light?

Let us recall the context. "There was a man sent from God" (1:6). In the midst of fallen history, there is saving history, redemptive history, and the proffered grace of God. But to "as many as received him, to them gave he power to become the sons of God, even to them that believe on his name" (1:12).

Even the Greeks say, "Sir, we would see Jesus" (12:21).

Even in the Sanhedrin, Nicodemus rises to his defense, saying, "Doth our law judge any man, before it hear him, and know what he doeth?" (7:51).

Even the centurion at Calvary owns him to be the Son of God (Mark 15:39).

Even when impaled upon the Cross, he establishes a new family on the basis of redemption rather than of human blood. "Woman, behold thy son! . . . Behold thy mother!" (19:26-27).

Even after the last blow has been struck against the Son of God, the crucified Christ rises in triumph from the tomb.

"The light shines on in the dark, and the darkness has never quenched it." Even here and now, God is at work in your life and mine, miserable sinners though we were, justifying us by his grace and sanctifying us by his power. "Christ in you, the hope of glory" (Col. 1:27). He answers our prayers, he promises strength sufficient in our weakness, and he pledges to conform us at last to his glorious image. "They shall see his face. . . . And there shall be no night there . . . for the Lord God giveth them light" (Rev. 22:4-5). "And the light shines on." Verily, the light shines forever.

## 48. The Compelling Motive
### REGINALD E. O. WHITE

•

The love of Christ constraineth us. 2 CORINTHIANS 5:14
We love him, because he first loved us. 1 JOHN 4:19

The constraining love which moves the Christian heart is no irrational emotion; Paul helps us to analyze its power.

I. It operates, Paul says, *upon the mind*, directing thought into new channels, erecting new standards of comparison, opening new worlds of ideas. "The love of Christ constraineth us; because we thus judge" that his death for us implies our death;

that if any man be in Christ he is a new creature; that all things are of God. In the light of the Cross all values are transfigured, all souls attain significance, all life is seen as open to redeeming intervention, the supreme tragedy as sin, the supreme folly, despair—since Jesus died for sinners. Thinking motivated by the Cross is the wisdom of God.

II. Constraining love operates, Paul says, *upon the will*, directing into new channels the driving energies of ambition and desire. The life that issued from self, controlled by the impulse to please oneself, justified and applauded by complacent self-approbation, is suddenly diverted, upwards "unto him," outwards unto others. At the Cross where we find ourselves for what we are, we also lost ourselves for what we may become. All great Christian lives show this odd characteristic of selflessness, puzzling and incredible to the non-Christian. They are too humble to think much of themselves, too meek to assert themselves, too grateful to pity themselves, too generous to better themselves at others' expense—yet they get things done. "He died for all, that they which live should not henceforth live unto themselves, but unto him" (2 Cor. 5:15).

III. The constraint operates, too, Paul says, *upon the heart*, and operates as love always must, with exclusive power. He must "have the preeminence" (Col. 1:18). Body, mind, time, talent, money, strength, life are his, first and only, for love's sake. The heart is made "a new creature," and looks out upon a world where "all things are of God" (2 Cor. 5:18), and feels impelled to break the alabaster of life over his dear feet, and protest through tears of penitence, joy, and love, "Lord, thou knowest that I love thee" (John 21:15). That is the compelling motive alone sufficient for Christian character, endurance, and service. Within the shadow of his Cross the risen Christ, at each memorial Supper, still confronts disciples with the wistful, searching plea, "Lovest thou, *lovest* thou me?"

## 49. The Four Gospels in Four Words

LOWELL M. ATKINSON

•

If we live in the Spirit, let us also walk in the Spirit. GALATIANS 5:25

To find the secret of full, rich, strong, confident, and abundant life is the great quest of the twentieth century. In a time that has been more bedeviled with crises and catastrophes than any other in the history of the modern world, more and more people seem increasingly unable to remain courageous and confident. So the Christian Gospel comes to us with its mighty message of hope, promise, and challenge: "If we live in the Spirit, let us also walk in the Spirit."

Life's crises are transfigured into dangerous but thrilling opportunities when we confront them courageously in the fullness of faith. Isaac Watts in a hymn much esteemed by John Wesley asks:

> And shall we then forever live
> At this poor dying rate?

It is indeed a question whether people are living or slowly dying. And what of ourselves? Shall we then forever live at this poor dying rate? The Gospel promises life abundant, if we have the Spirit working in us. It challenges us to live in faith and to walk worthy of the faith we enjoy. "Faith is our feet wherewith we walk to Christ. Love is our hands wherewith we do his will." How can we give the Four Gospels in four words? The Four Gospels present a single gospel of fullness of life in and through Christ. We shall sum it up in four words.

I. *Admit.* New life begins when we admit Jesus Christ into the place of authority and control in our hearts. It begins with decision and with personal dedication—the giving of ourselves to the Savior. Life begins when we accept God's promise of salvation provided through Jesus Christ.

II. *Submit.* This means you must humble yourself under the mighty hand of God. It means consecration. Christ must be Lord *of* all if he is to be Lord *at* all. Every area of life must come under his inspection, supervision, and guidance. In the light of his truth our spirits are humbled, and we know our need of repentance. But to submit to God, to be humble, to bow down in prayer, to give sincere expression to a real need of the soul, and to admit helplessness in the presence of the invading evil—this is hard to do and many do not do it. Blessed indeed are the poor in spirit, those who know the inner meaning of humility and submit their lives to Christ.

III. *Commit.* If we live in the Spirit, that is, if we admit Christ as our Savior and if we submit ourselves in consecration to him, then let us also walk in the Spirit. Now the inner life is expressed in our outer life. To commit our way unto the Savior means that he becomes not only our Savior from sin but our Guide in daily living. David Livingstone said, "Without him not one step, but with him anywhere." This is the meaning of the committed life. "If any man will come after me, let him deny himself, and take up his cross, and follow me" (Matt. 16:24).

IV. *Transmit.* Our life in Christ is incomplete if we have only admitted Christ into our life, submitted ourselves to him, and committed our way unto the Lord, Completion is possible only as we transmit the glories that have been revealed to us. The living Christ in our hearts must be expressed in word, purpose, and deed. A life of faith is a life of service. We enter the church to worship; we depart to serve. It is impossible for the Christian to enjoy the good things of the Gospel without seeking to share them. We share because we care. Because God has so loved us, we must tell of the wonderful story of his love. The essence of our Gospel is that it is a gospel for all the world. The faithful are commissioned to transmit the Good News of salvation.

These four words are the essential pillars of the saving truth that comes from the New Testament. They represent the verities by which we can live with confidence and strength, not at a poor dying rate, but with that fullness of life wherein faith works through love and wherein our spirit is made strong in hope.

## 50. Words for Living

LANCE WEBB

•

The Word was made flesh, and dwelt among us. JOHN 1:14

Words are terrible or wonderful things. They may wound and destroy, or heal and bless. For we live by speaking and by being spoken to. Words are bridges between us and others, including God, the word we use to describe the deepest meaning and the central reality of the universe.

The Bible describes man listening for God's word and trying to understand what he is saying. All that exists declares God's word in action, but his deeper word in meaning is declared by the prophets and supremely by our Lord.

With thankfulness we celebrate in the Lord's Supper God's word of action made flesh in his life, death, and resurrection—represented by the bread and the cup—and the word of meaning interpreting what he is thus saying to us.

The single most important factor in life is this ability to listen and communicate with each other, to be able to say in the words of a boy in a recent off-Broadway play, "Papa talked to me." Some of the saddest words ever uttered are "I can't get through to her" or "She doesn't understand me and I can't understand her." The boy's father had said, "We must listen carefully." So we must listen carefully, not only to each other, but supremely to God, for he is speaking to us. This is the reason for the Service of Communion, which might also be called a Service of Communication. We believe God has spoken to us the word of life in his Son. And in the Holy Spirit he speaks to us at his table if we listen to him.

Three of God's words for living spoken to us through Christ are *Come, Believe,* and *Go.*

I. The first word was spoken most clearly by Jesus, not only in what he said, but in what he was and did. Through the Gospel we hear God's invitation given not only to the disciples but also to the sick, the blind, the dumb, and to every one of us wherever we are: *"Come* unto me all you who are tired and weary, whose lives lack meaning, and I will give you life, rest, peace, joy, and power to become the sons of God." *(See* Matt. 11:28; John 10:10, 14:2, and 15:11.) These are truly the things which, above all else, we long for.

Of course, the wonderful words of life may be ruined by their misuse. It is only when we listen and hear these words in right relationship with God that we find true rest, real peace, creative joy, and life.

Without coming to him, these words are empty. For instance, totalitarian propaganda says, "Come to us and we will give you peace, plenty, and life." Or advertising merchants selling cosmetics, alcohol, and cigarettes say, "Come to us and we will give you love and joy!" The one kind of propaganda is as fulsome and false as the other.

II. Whom then can we believe? There must be something we can depend on. We desperately need Jesus' second word for living: "Have faith in God" (Mark 11:22). The key to finding life in him is to believe, not mental assent only, but acceptance and trust, a commitment leading to action.

III. Then we may hear the third great word for living—go. We have learned a new meaning of this word from the astronauts. When everything is working and in order for a space trip, the word is "Go!" Jesus' last words before his physical departure from his disciples sounded the same note: Now that you have the key in my life and victory, "Go . . . and teach all nations" (Matt. 28:19).

When God's word is understood and accepted, the next thing

required is to share it. If God is love and we love each other, there is a way to communicate with each other and even with those who are confused and lost and thus to help them over the tragedy of meaninglessness and confusion.

This is our supreme mission in life. Surely the only way effectively to meet the empty words of communist promises or even the-more-acceptable-to-us promises of a siren materialism is to say the words that represent the reality of God's truth and to back them up with ours. These words are "the Word is made flesh again." Every person is a word made flesh. What word are you? A word of selfishness and prejudice incarnate, or a word of truth and love?

If Christ is the meaning of your life, if you have come to God through him, if you believe, then you are ready to go. Not as a little, frantic self trying to play God, but as one who shares with others the most priceless things of life.

Come, believe, go—and live!

## 51. How God Handles Us

JAMES MOFFATT

•

And therefore will the Lord wait, that he may be gracious unto you, and therefore will he be exalted, that he may have mercy upon you: for the Lord is a God of judgment: blessed are all they that wait for him. ISAIAH 30:18

*And therefore.* In the Old Testament these are generally ominous words; like the short, heavy drops of rain that usher in a thunderstorm, they suggest some threat of punishment or doom to follow. But once or twice in the prophecies of Isaiah they introduce a promise, and so it is here. *And therefore,* the prophet tells the people, because of your extremity, on account of the sad pass to which you have brought yourselves by willfulness, *therefore* God will have pity on you in your plight; he will not repay hastiness by hastiness. The divine method of handling men is to let them feel the weight of their own misdoing now and then, until they realize their mistake, but never to let them go. The Lord does not say to his rebellious creatures, "Let them take the consequences of their sins; I am done with them." He says, "I will wait—I must let them alone till they come to themselves, till they are ready in shame to welcome my offer of guidance and control."

There is order and patience in God's dealing with our nature. We are not always so patient with one another. Punishment, indeed, is sometimes too hasty; a swift blow, a quick word, sharp irritation ending perhaps in estrangement, when things have begun to go wrong between one and another. Yes, but we sometimes forget that kindness may be hasty also. There are cases in which people are not ready as yet to be treated wisely with favor; they cannot understand generosity or receive help till they have gone through a phase of discipline; you must wait till they come to their senses before you can do them much permanent good. In our human ties, we need now and then to give people time, if they are to come right. Now often it takes time for us to become susceptible to God, and his glory is that he gives us time. It is his goodness that leads us to repentance— a wise goodness that knows exactly when we are in a condition to hear his voice, and knows how to bring us into that condition. God gives us time; he can wait, and he does wait.

But, you say, the prophet calls him *a God of judgment*! Does not that contradict this explanation? Some of you may even recall Watts's famous picture of "Time, Death, and Judgment," where Judgment is a robed figure with scales in one hand and a sword of fire; you recall how the painter has put under the picture this very text, "The Lord is a God of judgment: blessed are all they that wait for him." But that is a wrong interpretation, for when Isaiah declares that *the Lord is a God of judgment* he is stating a promise, not a somber threat. This is a word of deep encouragement. *Judgment* would be better rendered by "order" or "method" here. The phrase does not allude to any legal verdict of condemnation; it is a protest against the pagan notion of deity as capricious or arbitrary. *The Lord is a God of judgment* is the prophet's way of saying that he is never hasty; he acts steadfastly and loyally toward his people, even when they try his patience. The Lord whom we know fulfills all his duties toward us, and is never liable to gusts of exasperation or to fits of emotional pity. He deals regularly with men, neither yielding to some impulse of weak affection nor giving way to sudden fits of impatience, like pagan gods whose worshipers could not calculate upon their humors. He treats us with equal care and patience, whether his discipline requires to be exercised in severity or gentleness.

## 52. Happiness through Purity

BILLY GRAHAM

•

Blessed are the pure in heart: for they shall see God. MATTHEW 5:8

The heart is considered in Scripture far more than a bodily organ. It is called the seat of the emotions. Fear, love, courage, anger, joy, sorrow, and hatred are ascribed to the heart. It has come to stand for the center of the moral, spiritual, and intellectual life of a man. It is said to be the seat of a man's conscience and life.

Jesus said, "Happy are the pure in heart." Now, we should be able to take that for just what it means. If the heart is the seat of the affections, then our love toward God must be pure. If the heart is the center of our motives, then our motives must be pure. If the heart is the residence of our will, then our will must be yielded to Christ. We are to be pure in love, pure in motive, and pure in desire.

I. God does not judge the superficial goodness or the superficial badness that we do. He goes deeper into the soul and probes as a surgeon! When God is through probing our hearts, he says, "The heart is deceitful above all things, and desperately wicked: who can know it?" (Jer. 17:9).

When Jesus had finished probing the hearts of the people with whom he came in contact, he said, "Out of the heart of men proceed evil thoughts, adulteries, fornications, murders, thefts, covetousness, wickedness, deceit, lasciviousness, an evil eye, blasphemy, pride, foolishness" (Mark 7:21-22). Jesus taught that the human heart was far from God: darkened, unbelieving, blind, proud, rebellious, idolatrous, and stony. He taught that the human heart in its natural state is capable of any wickedness and any crime.

Our hearts are impure! As a result, we are filled with inner tension, pride, frustration, confusion, and a thousand and one other spiritual, mental, and physical ills. The very root of our lives is bad.

Jesus says we will never be completely and supremely happy until our hearts are pure.

II. This heart purity is not produced by mental suggestion, by environment, or by education. It is a miracle wrought by God himself. The Bible says, "A new heart also will I give you, and a new spirit will I put within you: and I will take away the stony heart out of your flesh" (Ezek. 36:26).

Purity of heart is a result of a rebirth, a miracle, a new creation. As the Bible says, "Which were born, not of blood, nor of the will of the flesh, nor of the will of man, but of God" (John 1:13).

You need a cleansed, forgiven, justified, new heart! Such can be received only as an act of God on the ground of the death of Christ on the Cross. When we have properly confessed and renounced our sins and by faith received Christ into our hearts, then we receive a new heart from God. Only then can we be called "pure in heart." Only then can we know the secret of happiness!

III. Have you received a new heart? It is impossible to live pure lives until we have pure hearts. If you have received a cleansed and pure heart from God, you are expected to live a pure life. Theologically, this is called "sanctification."

Pure hearts will be Christlike. It is God's desire that we be conformed to the image of his Son. If Christ lives within us and our bodies become the abode of the Holy Spirit, is it any wonder that we should be like him?

The Bible says, "Let this mind be in you, which was also in Christ" (Phil. 2:5). Jesus had a humble heart. If he abides in us, pride will never dominate our lives. Jesus had a loving heart. If he dwells within us, hatred and bitterness will never rule us. Jesus had a forgiving and understanding heart. If he lives within us, mercy will temper our relationships with our fellow men. Jesus had an unselfish heart. If he lives in us, selfishness will not predominate but service to God and others will come before our selfish interests.

You say, "That's a big order!" I admit that. It would be impossible if you had to measure up to him in your own strength and with your natural heart.

Paul recognized that he could never attain this heart purity by his own striving. He said, "I can do all things *through* Christ which strengtheneth me" (Phil. 4:13).

God hasn't left you alone, out on a limb! Jesus said to his disciples, "Lo, I am with you alway, even unto the end of the world" (Matt. 28:20). They did what they did because he was with them. They were nothing but a group of rough, unlettered men; but with Christ in their hearts they "turned the world upside down" (Acts 17:6).

Do you want to be happy? All right, apply this beatitude to your heart. Take it to yourself. The pure in heart are the only ones who can know what it means to be supremely happy. Their hearts are pure toward God and, as a result, are pure toward their fellow men. But the greatest happiness that comes to the pure in heart is not only a proper relationship with men but a sublime relationship with God. "For they shall see God." The gates of Eden swing open once more. God and man walk together once again.

## 53. Commanded to Be Glad

### Karl A. Olsson

•

Rejoice in the Lord alway: and again I say, Rejoice. PHILIPPIANS 4:4

We Christians are commanded to rejoice. This seems odd. We could understand better an exhortation to endure and to suffer. For these we would rather not do, and like soldiers, we do them only when we must. But to be glad is the heart's desire of nearly everyone.

Men cannot endure, as men, without gladness, and it is the intent of the Gospel, not to frustrate joy, but to give it a character and a source which do not fail. We are commanded to rejoice in the Lord—always. It is possible to misunderstand this and to do funny things with it. There is a Jesus mysticism which drowns itself in the sad, luminous eyes and the ashy face of the Veronica Christ. There is a Jesus liturgy which lives coldly in the aesthetic distortions of the crucifix. There is a morality which reduces Christ to a vendor of maxims. There is an evangelism so mechanical that it makes a personal encounter with the Lord impossible.

I. To rejoice in the Lord is something better than this. It is to yield to a miracle—to permit the Holy Spirit to re-enact the drama of salvation in me. To rejoice in the Lord is to follow the falling star—to see the Lord high and lifted up so that his glory fills the temple and to see him humbled for me and my salvation: the King become a slave; magnificence drained out in grubbiness; Divine Wisdom laughed at as folly; the good and wise Man—the Teacher in Israel, he who delights in the law of the Lord and meditates upon it day and night, the shining One who heals the sick and blesses children—this Man vilified, abused, ridiculed, lashed, and nailed up like a scarecrow on a stick. It is to feel all this in my bone-marrow and in my belly and to know that I am in it and that every horror of mine has nailed him where he is and is in turn nailed with him. It is to know that as his life drains from him, my sin drains from me. He has become sin for me; he has become my sin. My unmanageable me, so tense, so pettily selfish, so greedy, so devious, so inconstant, so truly horrible, is hammered up with him forever and forever. "Cursed is everyone that hangeth on a tree" (Gal. 3:13). He is cursed by what I am; I am blessed by having it identified with him in the indignity of the Cross. To rejoice in the Lord is to see him thus.

II. To rejoice in him is also to see his exaltation and to know it as a resurrecting earthquake which shakes this tenement of grass. It is to rise with him. O blessed and impenetrable mystery! It is to lay aside the graveclothes of my dying self. Who has not trembled before the death catalogues in Colossians 3: anger, slander, foul talk, immorality, impurity, passion? Who has not been moved to gladness by the new garments of the resurrection: compassion, kindness, lowliness, meekness, patience?

We need an image. The resurrection is an April morning with the dead winter dying in every shaded place and the new grass cold and green around the daffodils. It is time to roll up and put away our old ragged trousers or the spotted dress and the shoes with the flapping soles; it is time to put on our Easter clothes. It is time to be kissed by the sun and to buy violets and to love all that is lovable. "Arise, my love, my fair one, and come away; for lo, the winter is past, the rain is over and gone. The flowers appear on the earth, the time of singing has come, and the voice of the turtledove is heard in our land" (S. of S. 2:10-12, RSV).

III. To rejoice in the Lord is to be made over. It is not only to find something to be glad about; it is also to enter into the joy of the Lord. It is to share in the rapture which lifts us from the burning marl of our transgression into his presence. To rejoice in the Lord is to be on our way out of the City of Destruction and out of Vanity Fair, and never to return. To rejoice is to be under authority and to heed a command.

## 54. Has Your Life Divine Direction?

WILLIAM McLEISTER, 2ND

●

> After he had seen this vision we at once set about getting a passage to Macedonia, concluding that God had called us to bring them the good news. ACTS 16:10, NEB

We cannot read far in the Book of Acts without concluding that the infant Church was specifically, definitely, and directly guided by God through the Holy Spirit in its decisions, plans, and strategy. Paul and his companions were conscious of God's guidance.

Do we not possess the same Holy Spirit? Is not God's power also available to us? Are not our plans as important to God as were those of the Apostle and his associates? And more specifically, can we not also have a sense of God's guidance in our individual lives?

The passage from which the text comes indicates ways by which we may learn what constitutes God's will for us.

I. *Consideration.* The sixteenth chapter of Acts points to three times when God specifically led the apostles. The Holy Spirit "forbade" the preaching of the gospel in Asia; the Spirit of Jesus "prevented" Paul from going into Bithynia; and one night at Troas Paul had a vision in which a Macedonian called, saying, "Come across to Macedonia and help us."

In response, did Paul simply come to a snap decision? Not at all. He carefully considered all the factors relating to that important step. He called, as we might say, a committee meeting with Silas, Timothy, and Luke. After prayer, they undertook to examine the facts. The Authorized Version reads, "assuredly gathering that the Lord had called us." How did they get that assurance? The Greek word literally means "to bring together," "to lay side by side," "to compare," or "to consider."

Their method commends itself to us. We shall come to meaningful decisions when, having sought through prayer for evidence of God's will, we carefully plan on the basis of available considerations.

II. *Commitment.* The factor of commitment is closely associated with consideration. I should think that commitment logically both precedes and follows consideration.

George Mueller, when writing on "How I Ascertain the Will of God," placed consecration in the prior place. To find the will of God for our lives, we must lose our own wills. This means commitment. If God shows his will to you, will you do it? God will not reveal his will to us if we are not ready to do it. Commitment is the necessary prerequisite to getting God's guidance.

And commitment follows consideration, for having carefully considered the implications of a plan of action, there comes the moment when we must willingly throw caution to the winds and, if necessary, step out and do what we sincerely believe to be God's will, whatever the considerations. We read concerning Paul and his colleagues that after the vision, "at once we set about." Delayed action following a decision is the father of disobedience. When God shows us something to do, we will not do it if we unnecessarily delay.

III. *Confirmation.* Luke records that the apostles had "a straight run"—a smooth journey—from Troas to the port of Philippi. The winds blew favorably to the port of call for those who had undertaken to do God's will. God's confirmation of his will does not mean, however, that God will always or even usually spare us from suffering and hardship. The opposite more often seems to be true, for committed Christians know the swelling of Jordan and must pass through deep places of suffering.

Yet there is a confirmation that attends the undertaking of the will of God for our lives. Though outward conditions may seem perilous, the obedient Christian experiences peace, poise, and power within. This confirmation more frequently is seen in retrospect and not in prospect. At any given moment we may not be certain that God is confirming his will, but as we continue in faith there come insights and understandings that God's purposes are being fulfilled in our lives and we glimpse on some distant height foregleams of victory. This requires great faith, but ours is a religion of faith and God calls us to grasp anew the guidance and providence he offers.

## 55. Delight in the Will of God

JOHN A. BROADUS

•

I delight to do thy will, O my God. PSALM 40:8

This psalm tells of one who has suffered, been graciously relieved, and now responds in grateful praise and grateful obedience. This is not shown by mere externals of worship, but by delighting to do God's will, by having his law in the heart, by proclaiming his glorious character and gracious dealings (verses 1-10).

Verses 5-9 apply to Christ. So it is with various psalms; often the language is exclusively prophetic of him. These words, therefore, are designed to be adopted by anyone, while at the same time it may look to the great example of the Lord Jesus

Christ. Observe, that this delight is not merely to hear, but to do, the will of God.

I. In one sense, the will of God will always be done, whether we do his will or not.

Here we touch a most difficult subject but we need not turn away from it; but we must be humble, and content to take what we can understand, and leave alone what we cannot.

We are compelled to speak of God's will in terms applicable to our own. This is done in Scripture. There are three distinct senses in which this term is employed. First, the will of purpose; it is always done. "Who worketh all things after the counsel of his own will" (Eph. 1:11). "He doeth according to his will in the army of heaven, and among the inhabitants of the earth" (Dan. 4:35). Next, the will of desire, or wish, which is not always done—for inscrutable reasons he permits free agents to act counter to his wish. "How often would I have gathered thy children together . . . and ye would not!" (Matt. 23:37). "Who will have all men to be saved, and to come unto the knowledge of the truth" (1 Tim. 2:4). Last, will of command—the wish of one in authority, when expressed, becomes a command. Every command of God it is our solemn duty to obey—but, alas! it is not always done. Of course, it is human imperfection that makes these distinctions necessary, and they must not be pushed too far—yet they are, within limits, just distinctions, and should be borne in mind.

Now God's purpose, as distinguished from other senses, is not dependent upon us for accomplishment. It may be accomplished without us, by overruling and finding others willing. But God's will of desire, what is well-pleasing to him, we should seek to ascertain, and do. His will of command we should learn and obey.

How do we ascertain what is God's will? Partly from our own conscience, aided by general conscience of mankind, but this is by no means an infallible exponent of God's will. What has come to pass—is always in accordance with God's general purpose, however wrong the motives of agents—gives indication as to what we should do. To some extent we may seek the best judgment and advice of others. It is always important to have the mind stored with Scripture. Then we can pray and trust we are doing God's will.

II. We should always do God's will, even if it be not with delight.

We seldom, if ever, do anything with perfectly correct motives and feelings. Yet with the most proper sentiments we can at the time command, let us still do our duty.

Sometimes we cannot rise above resignation. Especially when we have to bear what disappoints and distresses us.

Sometimes we may do his will with shrinking and reluctance. Human nature is weak. Even apart from sin, it naturally shrinks from danger, suffering, physical or mental. Even Jesus, to whom the text specially applied. "And what shall I say? Father, save me from this hour: but . . ." (John 12:27). Again, "If it be possible . . . nevertheless not as I will, but as thou wilt" (Matt. 26:39). This cost an effort, and a struggle, for a time—yet he did not fail to do it.

Yes, we should always do God's will, even if it is not a delight. And often, the painful effort will change to pleasure, the duty commenced reluctantly will become a sweet joy!

Yet, do not condition obedience upon its becoming delightful. It is the will of my God? Then his will I must do.

III. We should delight to do God's will.

We may be led to it.

1. By sense of right. The vexing question of ethical speculation does not here matter—whether God wills a thing because it is right, or it is right because he wills it. What he wills is right. To do right is man's highest duty, and should be his greatest delight.

2. By feelings of interest. It is right to consult our own improvement and enjoyment. Lawful to be pleased at advancing these, provided we are doing God's will. Now always our true

interest, in noblest sense, on largest scale, is to do God's will. Hence self-love should conspire with a sense of right in causing us to delight in God's will.

3. By feelings of benevolence. I hope no one present is wholly ignorant of the pleasure derived from benefiting others. "And learn the luxury of doing good" (Goldsmith). Now in doing God's will, we may be sure we are promoting the well-being of our fellow men—whether we can always perceive the connection or not. If it is God's will, it shall be best for all we love, for all mankind, that this should be done. What a pleasure, then, it should be, to do his will.

4. By feelings of gratitude. My brethren, let us think of all our providential and spiritual blessings. And while our hearts glow with gratitude, for all God has done, and is doing, and promises to do for us, shall we not be able to say, "I delight to do thy will, O my God"?

In doing God's will, we follow the example of Jesus—seen in his whole life, and declared in his own words. Remember him at Jacob's well—fatigued, needing rest and food, yet busy doing good, and yet saying to his disciples, "My meat is to do the will of him that sent me, and to finish his work" (John 4:34). In doing this, we are dear to Jesus. "Whosoever shall do the will of my Father which is in heaven, the same is my brother, and sister, and mother" (Matt. 12:50). We become as near as the dearest kindred.

# 56. Vows

HERBERT H. FARMER

•

> I will pay my vows unto the Lord now in the presence of all his
> people. PSALM 116:14

I. Vows should be made at the right time. "I will pay my vows
*now.*" What then is the right time, the supreme "now" for
vow-making? It is surely the time when for one reason or another there comes to you an unusual moment of higher vision
and desire; when something in your inner life as it were stirs
and lifts you for a little above the routine, above the trivialities
and superficialities of things, and you become aware of the
greatness and seriousness of the issues of life, and the dignity of
personal being that might be achieved by dealing with them in
a greathearted and serious way. Then and there, if you are
wise, at that so swiftly passing "now" of high feeling, you will
pause, and summoning all that is within you, you will seek to
harness the mood to the deepest and most central thing in your
personal being, which is your will, that is to say you will seek
to harness it to what is in essence a vow. The true vow is the
attempt to capture the high and serious moment, to take it out
of the transiencies and make it one of the permanencies of the
soul's life, to condense out of the vapor of feeling a solid mass
and momentum of directed will.

II. The vow should be made in the right company. "I will
pay my vows . . . now *in the presence of all his people.*"

The solitary vow, however earnest, is the weak vow and
already half-defeated. It is weak because there is no check upon
the vanity and extravagance and self-reference which can creep
into even the highest mood. No mood is so high but that it
needs a salting of sanity and common sense, such as often can
only come from a community experience wider and bigger than

our own. It is weak because there is no sustaining atmosphere, no supporting environment, no continuous feeding and nourishing and educating of the whole being in the direction of its highest feelings and insights. It is weak because there is lacking the strengthening and rebuking expectancies of one's fellows. Down to the very roots of our being, and therefore up to its highest fruits, we are social beings; we live and move and have our being, far more than we realize, in one another. It is surely not something to be wholly ashamed of to say that more than once it has been the thought of my friends, the sense of having made vows in their presence, which has kept my feet from straying. I conceive that God may lay his hand upon us through our fellows, seeing that he has bound us in such close bonds to our fellows.

III. The vow must be paid to the right person. "I will pay my vows *unto the Lord.*"

In any worthy vow there must be a deep and recollected sense of God. If we need to drive the stake of a vow into the flux of the soul's life in order, as it were, to tether our visions to it, we also need something to enable us to drive that stake firmly in. And that something is the thought of God and his absolute will.

# VII
# THE FELLOWSHIP
# OF
# THE REDEEMED

# 57. Why Be a Christian?

JAMES S. STEWART

•

Who is like unto thee, O people saved by the Lord? DEUTERONOMY
33:29

Is there not something like the sound of a trumpet in that?
Here surely is a word of God to stir and thrill our hearts.

For you see what it does. It takes religion, the life that is lived
for God, it takes (to bring this right over without delay into
the light of the Gospel revelation) the life in Christ, and it lifts
it up before the eyes of the world, and cries, "There—can you
beat that?" It takes a life which God has redeemed and blessed
and regenerated, any such life—it matters not where it is found,
whether in the courts of the house of the Lord, or in a garret
in a slum—it takes that life, and holds it high, and challenges
the world to produce anything like it. "Bring out your best," it
dares the world, "bring out your very best and highest—and see
how that Christ-redeemed life will dwarf it! For there, in the
humblest soul on which God has set his seal, is something that
you simply cannot achieve, cannot even touch—and never shall."
"Who is like unto thee, O people saved by the Lord?"

So declares the Word of God. Do we agree with it? Certainly
it is a daring challenge. It is a vast and sweeping claim. Do you
think it is perhaps too daring, too self-assured? Let us look into
it. Let us cross-question it. Let us come down to particulars

and ask: In what specific ways does the Christian life beat all the rest? Just how is it superior? Clearly if we can answer this question, the other question—Why be a Christian?—automatically answers itself.

First, I am prepared to maintain this, that the Christian life is *happier than any other*.

But I can imagine someone saying, "Is that an adequate motive? Might it not, indeed, be just a species of selfishness to embrace Christianity for the happiness it gives?" Clearly we must attempt a further answer. I ask you now to consider a second point, of a totally different kind. The Christian life is *harder than any other*.

Will you take now a third factor into consideration? The life in Christ is *holier than any other*.

One last claim let me make. The Christian life is *more hopeful than any other*.

It is a happier life than any other, a harder life, a holier life, an infinitely more hopeful life. Why be a Christian? Is anyone hesitating? Does someone need just one word more to carry him into the kingdom? Then let that word be this. It is not only a happy, a hard, a holy, a hopeful life. It is *his* life!

That is what you are being offered—the very life which Jesus lived, the very eternity where Jesus reigns forever. His life! And he is offering it to you himself. To you by name he offers it. Listen, when you say your prayers tonight. Listen, when you are alone, and the service of this hour is but a memory. Listen, when your soul is quiet. And it may be that, ringing clear through the dark, there will come a Voice, and you will hear him speak your name. And then—"Brother, sister," he will say, "I give you this—my life, my Spirit, my love and joy and peace, I give them all to you." What a day tomorrow would be if that happened between your soul and Christ tonight! And how radiant all life's tomorrows, until the last great daybreak come!

# 58. How to Be a Christian

HUGH THOMSON KERR

•

And it came to pass, that a whole year they assembled themselves with the church, and taught much people. And the disciples were called Christians first in Antioch. ACTS 11:26

It is possible to trace the word "Christian" to within ten years of the death of Christ. It is an unusual and provocative word. It has a Hebrew significance, a Greek formation, and a Latin ending. Like the title over the Cross, it was written in Hebrew, Greek, and Latin. The name "Christian" was given to the followers of Jesus neither by themselves nor by the Jews, but by the Greek-speaking people of Antioch. It was a nickname, a byword, and it was given in derision and contempt. Wherever we meet this word in the New Testament there is a sting in it; there is reproach and ridicule.

A distinctive name was given to designate a new species. The people of Antioch had many names in their resourceful language but they had no name to cover this type of character. These people did things, said things, lived things—lived things hitherto unheard of in the history of the world. They lived purity—purity of a new order, purity of thought and feeling. They lived forgiveness—forgiveness of a new kind, forgiveness for friend and foe alike. They lived love—love of a new order, love for all the world, for bond and free, rich and poor. They lived humility—humility new to the world, humility that was a reproach to the people, humility that made a friend of poverty and of workingmen and of slaves. These were the ideas they preached and taught and lived and glorified until they produced a new type of manhood and womanhood after the likeness of Jesus.

Years ago a German theologian, David Friedrich Strauss, published an article entitled "Are We Yet Christians?"; and the question is still provoking. Because of your Christian character would the men in your town need a new name by which to describe you? Because of the unselfishness of your disposition and the winsomeness of your character would you, who mingle in the social circles of the city, both claim and require the designation of a new name? Does your life demand the continuation of a distinctive name or must you wear a badge and recite a creed and herald your allegiance in order to be known as a Christian?

In a remarkable study of the life of Christ, *The Jesus of History*, T. R. Glover says:

The Christian proclaimed a war of religion in which there shall be no compromise and no peace, till Christ is Lord of all; the thing shall be fought out to the bitter end. And it has been. He was resolved that the old gods should go; and they have gone. How was it done? Here we touch what I think one of the greatest wonders that history has to show. How did the Church do it? If I may invent or adapt three words, the Christian "out-lived" the pagan, "out-died" him, and "out-thought" him. . . . The old religion crumbled and fell, beaten in thought, in morals, in life, in death. And by and by the only name for it was paganism, the religion of the back-country village, of the out-of-the-way places. Christ had conquered.

That victory of the early Church is our challenge, for their God is our God and his Spirit still broods over all. The challenging opportunity of the present is to demonstrate the transforming power of the Gospel; and in the spirit of him whom having not seen we love to bring in the new day of sweetness and light, of love and goodwill. This is our challenge and this is our call as Christians.

# 59. Live a Lighted Life

LESLIE CONRAD, JR.

•

*Let your light so shine before men, that they may see your good works and give glory to your Father who is in heaven.* MATTHEW 5:16, RSV

Light, especially in the Scriptures, is a fascinating phenomenon. In the first chapter of the first book of the Bible, light is listed as God's first creation. In the last chapter of the last book of the Bible, in the very last verse of John the Beloved's revelatory vision, he writes of light, "And night shall be no more; they need no light of lamp or sun, for the Lord God will be their light, and they shall reign for ever and ever" (Rev. 22:5, RSV).

Between these two mighty enlightening verses, Holy Writ is radiant with guidance on "how to live a lighted life." More than all else, the Light of Life, Jesus the Christ, offers the most valuable advice.

Jesus summed up his mission to mankind in one sentence, "I am the light of the world" (John 8:12). Jesus did not say, "I am the light of Americans or Caucasians or Republicans." He did not say, "I am the light of Lutherans or Presbyterians or Methodists." He did not say, "I am the light of the well-bred or the well-read or the well-fed."

Jesus emphatically stressed, "I am the light of the world"! He is the spiritual light for every land and for every person in every land. But Jesus also stated in his Sermon on the Mount, "Ye are the light of the world" (Matt. 5:14). Christ's aim for his follower is that he live a lighted life. *Your* light must be *his* light.

In an effort to put more Christlike light into your life, consider as aids some of the common characteristics of light.

I. The first characteristic is that light travels in straight lines. Do you recall the old Mother Goose rhyme?

> There was a crooked man, and he went a crooked mile,
> He found a crooked sixpence beside a crooked stile.
> He bought a crooked cat, which caught a crooked mouse,
> And they all lived together in a little crooked house.

The light of Jesus Christ cannot shine through a crook. The light of Jesus Christ has no crooked properties or processes. The light of Jesus Christ glows straight!

When Jesus said, "I am the light of the world," he must have meant, "I believe in straight living, straight loving, straight walking, and straight talking, so straightly straight that no one who hears my words and watches my works will ever pursue a crooked path."

II. A second characteristic of light is its usefulness. Light is to be used. Of the Seven Wonders of the Ancient World, including the Pyramids of Egypt and the Hanging Gardens of Babylon, only the Lighthouse of Alexandria served a useful purpose. And, of course, firelight was the useful feature of that old-world wonder.

Jesus quite candidly described the usefulness of light when he advised his hearers that the proper place for a lighted candle is not under a bushel basket but on a candlestand.

III. Another characteristic of light is that the nearer you are to the light-source, the more light you have. The nearer you live to Christ, the more Christ-light beams forth from your own life.

IV. Furthermore, consider two processes by which light travels from its source: transmission and reflection. In this calling to lighted living, both processes may be employed. But of the two, a transparent transmitter of light is a great deal more worth while than a mere mirrorlike reflector.

Christ is the source of all true spiritual light; you are the channel; the source shines through the channel.

# 60. Walking in the Light

JAMES DENNEY

●

> If we walk in the light, as he is in the light, we have fellowship one
> with another, and the blood of Jesus Christ his Son cleanseth us
> from all sin. 1 JOHN 1:7

Light and darkness are words which the Apostle uses both in
the Fourth Gospel and in the epistle, but which he never explains. Partly they do not need explanation and partly they
do not admit of it. We feel the freedom with which they are
used when he says in one sentence that God is light, and in the
next that God is in the light. We feel that in some aspects light
and darkness might be regarded as equivalent to holiness and
sin, but the text itself is enough to show that they are not to be
simply identified.

The Christian conscious of sin is called by the Apostle to
walk in the light as God is in the light in order that the blood
of Jesus may cleanse him from all sin. What is suggested by
"light" throughout the passage is something absolutely luminous and transparent, in which there is no concealment and no
need for any. To say that God is light is to say for one thing
that in God there is nothing to hide: if he is dark, it is with
excess of brightness; it is because he dwells in light that is in-
accessible, not because there is anything in him which of its
own nature craves obscurity.

This is the line on which our thoughts are led by the following verses, where the opposite of walking in the light is evidently hiding sin, or denying that we have sinned. It is some
kind of secrecy—which no doubt has its motive in sin—that is
meant by darkness, and this gives us the key to walking in the
light. To walk in the light means to live a life in which there is
nothing hidden, nothing in which we are insincere with our-

selves, nothing in which we seek to impose upon others. We may have, and no doubt we will have, both sin and the sense of sin upon us—"If we say that we have no sin, we deceive ourselves, and the truth is not in us" (1 John 1:8) —but we may walk in the light nevertheless, if we deal truly with our sin, and it is only as we do so that we enjoy Christian fellowship and are cleansed by the blood of Jesus. What, then, is specially required of us if we would walk in the light?

I. It requires in the first place prompt confession of sin. The sin that lies upon the conscience unconfessed darkens the whole moral being. But to confess is not the first impulse when we have sinned. Pride, fear, shame, and other powerful feelings keep us back. Our first impulse is to hide our sin, or rather to ignore it; to try to believe that the best that can now be done is to forget it, and to go on as if it had never been; to brace ourselves up to bear the inevitable consequences as stoically as we can; in any case, to say nothing about it, in the hope that in time it may work itself out, and that God will say nothing about it either. The 32nd Psalm, which tells the story of a penitent and pardoned sinner, begins verse 3 with the words, "When I kept silence." That is the first impulse. But to keep silence is to walk in the dark and to walk alone. The unconfessed sin separates us from God, and from all his redeeming and cleansing power. Of course he knows it, but it is not enough that he should know, it is necessary that we should tell him. If we are going to walk in the light, there must be no shunning of God's presence, no restraint of prayer, no hiding of anything from him even for an hour.

II. Further, to walk in the light means that we confess our sins without reserve. Sometimes we do not really confess when we think we are doing so: we rather admit our sins than confess them, and we seek in all possible ways to explain, to extenuate, and to excuse them. We may confess them in words, but in the secret of our hearts we do not take blame; we do not admit full responsibility for them. We think of the evil nature we have inherited, of the bias in our constitution to this or that attractive vice, of the defects of our education, of the violence of temptation, of the compulsion of circumstances; we do not deny what we have done—we cannot—but we mitigate it by every possible plea. This is not walking in the light. In all such self-excusing there is a large element of voluntary self-deception which keeps the life in the dark. To walk in the light requires us to accept our responsibilities without reserve, to own our sin that we may be able to disown it, and not to own it with such qualifications and reserves as amount to saying in the long run, It was indeed I who did it, but after all it is not I who should bear the blame. A man who makes it his business not to confess his sin, but to understand and to explain it, no matter how philosophical he may seem, is walking in darkness, and the truth is not in him. There is nothing in his attitude which gives him the benefit either of fellowship with Christians or of the cleansing blood of Jesus.

III. Finally, to walk in the light means that when we confess our sins to God we do not keep a secret hold of them in our hearts. Many a man confesses the sin he has done, and knows that he is going to do it again. It is not only in his nature to do it; it is in his inmost desire. He has been found out, exposed, humiliated, punished; yet he is saying to himself, "When I awake, I will seek it yet again." It need not be said that there is no hope here: this is the man who is shut up at last in the iron cage of despair, where there is something hidden in the heart, hidden from God and from man. The desire to keep such a secret hold of sin is itself a sin to be confessed, to be declared in its exceeding sinfulness, to be unreservedly renounced; and it is only when the life is brought into the light by such openness that the Christian experiences of which the Apostle speaks are put within its reach.

The man who has a guilty secret in his life is a lonely man. There can be no cordial Christian overflow from his heart to the hearts of others, nor from theirs to his. And he is a man doomed to bear in his loneliness the uneffaced stain of his sin. The cleansing virtue of the atonement cannot reach him where he dwells by himself in the dark. He is cut off from the two great blessings of the Gospel which are conditioned by walking in the light—the fellowship of Christians with one another, and the sanctifying power of the blood of Jesus.

## 61. The Church's Appeal to Men

### HUGH BLACK

Come thou with us, and we will do thee good. . . . Leave us not, I pray thee; forasmuch as thou knowest how we are to encamp in the wilderness, and thou mayest be to us instead of eyes. NUMBERS 10:29, 31

At this point of the story of Israel, Moses and the rescued tribes have begun their wanderings through the desert. The future is full of difficulty and danger, though it is bright with the confidence of faith. Moses appeals to Hobab to share in that great future, to cast in his lot with them. "The Lord hath spoken good concerning Israel." The blessing will rest on all who belong to Israel. To share in the toil is to share in the reward, and the reward is sure. There is no hesitation in the offer to Hobab. It is plainly for his own good that he should accept it.

Hobab's reply was a refusal. Not perhaps because he did not believe in the future of Israel, but simply because he had other interests which seemed good enough for him without any further addition. He was content with his life as it was, and had sufficient interests already.

But Moses had another plea, even after this distinct refusal, a plea under the circumstances far more powerful to such a man than the offer of personal good. He could be their guide and their guardian, and could be a help to them of untold value. He might be as their very eyes.

I. This twofold argument is the appeal the Church makes to men. The Church says with assurance, "Come and we will do thee good; for the Lord hath spoken good concerning Israel." It says this with emphasis; it say it pleadingly. It has blessings, promises, and powers, of which it is sure. It knows that men are in need of what it possesses. It sees men living to little purpose and for little ends. It sees the sin and the sorrow. It has deep pity for the deep pathos of human life. Its whole work is to do men good, as it declares the Gospel of the kingdom, calling them to pardon and peace, offering them salvation, presenting to them the manifold riches of Christ, pointing to the way of life and of joy.

II. But there is another strand in the cord with which the Church would grapple you. It is a powerful argument to a high heart; and the Church's very existence—encamped in the wilderness, fighting the great battle against principalities and powers of evil, seeking, striving, suffering for that Promised Land, for man's higher life on earth, waiting for the consolation of Israel, giving itself to the great task of establishing the kingdom of heaven on earth—the Church's very existence is an appeal to you. God had spoken good concerning Israel whether Hobab came or stayed; but it was much to have Hobab's help in the great enterprise, much to have one who could be to them instead of eyes. And the kingdom of heaven will come with you or without you; but just because it is a task high and hard, you should be in the thick of it, taking your part of the glorious burden. Though you might not think of coming for your own sake, can you resist this other appeal to come for our sake?

# 62. The Church of Tomorrow

## GASTON FOOTE

Upon this rock I will build my church; and the gates of hell shall not prevail against it. MATTHEW 16:18

A nineteenth-century English essayist, passing a wayside crucifix, is reported to have muttered, "Poor fellow, he's about done for." Little could he imagine that this "Man upon a cross" is indelibly etched upon the minds of more men today than ever before.

A German philosopher of an earlier day wrote in substance, "God is dead. He laughed himself to death at man's stupidity in believing in the gods."

Religion, and particularly Christianity, has always had its critics. That is good, for no one is so disrespectful as to criticize a dead man or institution. So far, however, the Church has always witnessed the burial of its critics.

But what of the Church of tomorrow? How may it be made a more effective force of Divine redemption in a decadent world?

I. The Church of tomorrow must be redeemed from pessimism to optimism. When churchmen of today become pessimistic, they shoud read once again the story of the first-century Church. We read of the miracles in the Bible. Consider the miracle of the Church itself! Amid such opposition, how did it ever survive? The Apostle Paul, himself a martyr, wrote what we might call his signature tune or theme song: "Finally, my brethren, rejoice in the Lord" (Phil. 3:1). The early Christians found much to rejoice over. Their Lord was alive forevermore. Every Sabbath was for them an Easter morning. They went to their executions with songs on their lips. They rejoiced in their tribulations.

166

There is too much pessimism in the contemporary Church. We often act as though God were a memory and powerless to show his mighty works today. We look back at what God did rather than forward to what God can do. We preach about punishment for sins. But that is only half of our gospel. We must also preach of the power, through God, to overcome them.

In one of our churches there is a large candelabrum having sixty-six lights which represent the books of the Bible. The minister's son, seeing that one of the lights was out, said, "Daddy, Lamentations is out." Well, it ought to be out! For too long we have been singing "Hold the Fort" when we should be singing "Onward, Christian Soldiers."

II. The Church of tomorrow must be redeemed from competition to co-operation. The forces of evil are too great to be opposed by a divided Church. By a united Church we do not mean a supercolossal ecclesiastical machine. We seek not uniformity but unity of purpose. Freedom is our finest word and if we lose the freedom to worship as we see fit we endanger other freedoms as well.

We seek unity of the Christian conscience of the world because "God wills it." We Christians have a common heritage: "One Lord, one faith, one baptism" (Eph. 4:5). We have a common enemy. The forces of secularism, nihilism, and godless totalitarianism are united against us. We have a common responsibility, "Go ye therefore, and teach all nations, baptizing them in the name of the Father, and of the Son, and of the Holy Ghost" (Matt. 28:19).

We have spent too much time defending our differences and too little time in discovering the basis of our unity. Skeptical men will not be convinced of the validity of the Christian faith until we are bound together by the indissoluble love of our common Lord.

III. The Church of tomorrow must be redeemed from formalism to evangelism. The devil wages a two-pronged attack upon the Church: formalism, on the one hand, and fanaticism,

on the other. If he cannot drive us into the corner of unreason-
able fanaticism, he seeks to smother us with cold formality. An
appropriate sign for many of our churches reads, "Died of
Dignity."

The Church is the only institution among men whose primary business is to bring people into a redemptive relationship
with God. Service clubs, chambers of commerce, and public
schools cannot do this. Everything the Church does should
center in this compelling purpose. Nothing else really matters.

In *The Miracle Worker* the mother of blind, deaf, and mute
Helen Keller leans over the cradle of the little child and sobs,
"Don't you know that we would do anything on earth to help
you? Don't you know that we love you?" So the Church through
the centuries leans over the cradle of the blind, deaf, and silent
potential sons of God and sobs, "Don't you know that 'God so
loved the world, that he gave his only begotten Son, that whosoever believeth in him should . . . have everlasting life' " (John
3:16)?

# VIII
# OUR LIFE
# IN HIM

# 63. To Live Is Christ

HENRY DRUMMOND

●

For to me to live is Christ, and to die is gain. PHILIPPIANS 1:21

*We have all in some way made the discovery of Christ*—we know more about Christ than Paul did when he became a Christian. When he made him the center of his life, he knew less of him perhaps than most of us. It is a startling truth, at all events, that we are as near the center of life—the center of the universe—as Paul. We have heard of him from our infancy; the features of his life are as familiar as our own; we have no hatred to him as Paul had once. And if the few days' quietness in the Holy Land, which Paul had on the threshold of his change, were in any way a preparation for the crisis of his life, how much more has our past life been a preparation for a change in ours! We call Paul's change a sudden conversion— we do not know how sudden it was. But if our life was changed today, it would be no sudden conversion. Our preparation, so far as knowledge of the new center goes, is complete. The change, so far as that is concerned, might happen *now*. We have the responsibility of being so near eternal life as that.

The question comes to be simply a question of transfer. To me to live is myself, or to me to live is Christ. To live for Christ is not simply the sublime doctrine which it includes of *Christ our life*. It is not so much Christ our life, but rather *our life for Christ.*

Shall it be, then, our life for Christ? "To me to live is Christ." Contrast it with all the other objects of life; take all the centers out of all the great lives, and compare them one by one. Can you match the life-creed of Paul—"to me to live is Christ"?

"To me to live is—*business*," "to me to live is—*pleasure*," "to me to live is—*myself*." We can all tell in a moment what our religion is really worth. "To me to live is"—*what*? *What* are we living for? First thoughts, it is said, are best in matters of conscience. What was the first thought that came into our hearts just then?

"To me to live is business," "to me to live is pleasure," "to me to live is myself." What kind of an end to an immortal life is this? How much nobler a center our life is worthy of our life, our one precious life, which is to live forevermore; which is to live with a great center or a mean one—meanly or greatly forevermore.

The time will come when we shall ask ourselves why we ever crushed this infinite substance of our life within these narrow bounds, and centered that which lasts forever on what must pass away. In the perspective of eternity all lives will seem poor, and small, and lost, and self-condemned beside a life for Christ. There will be plenty then to gather round the Cross. But who will do it now? There are plenty of men to die for him, there are plenty to spend eternity with Christ; but where is the man who will *live* for Christ? Christ wants *lives*. No fear about death being again if we have lived for Christ. There is but one alternative—the putting on of Christ; Paul's alternative, the discovery of Christ.

We have all in some sense, indeed, already made the discovery of Christ. We may be as near it now as Paul when he left Jerusalem. There was no notice given that he was to change masters. The new Master simply crossed his path one day, and the great change was come. How often has he crossed our path? Death can only be gain when to have lived was Christ.

# 64. What Does It Mean to Take God Seriously?

### HELMUT THIELICKE

•

It is impossible to "know" God by observing life and analyzing history and the like and then saying that, if we should find him in this way, then we will take him seriously, then we will be active in his cause and make him the standard of our life. It is just the opposite: only he who takes him seriously ever knows him at all. No one else ever knows him.

But how can one take him seriously when one knows nothing about him? Well, I should say that one should deal with God in exactly the same way that the nobleman dealt with his servants in the parable of the pounds. The nobleman said, "I will condemn you out of your own mouth" (Luke 19:22, RSV). In other words: I will meet you and discuss this with you on your own level. In exactly the same way we should say to God, "I will convict you by what you yourself have said. Let it be your own words that either convince me or with which I rout you and show up your absurdity. Here are your words: 'Cast all your cares on me, for I care for you.' Very well, I'll do this and test it out. I have some cares. I'm afraid of tomorrow and next week. This time I won't read my daily and weekly horoscope; instead I'll pour out my fears to you. I'll try you out, God, this once. You ought to be worth an experiment. I'll see whether you really can get me through tomorrow and next week. I'll find out whether you really will build paths for me when the going is hard, whether you really will put rod and staff in my hand in the dark valleys, whether you really will see to it that I do not lose trust in your guiding hand in the darkest moments when I cannot see either the bridge or the path, the shepherd or the staff."

To take God seriously means to take him at his word and to give him the opportunity to respond in the way he has promised to do in his Word. We can never receive anything with clenched fists or drooping arms. We must be willing to stretch out our hands and "open our mantle wide," as Luther once said.

Perhaps we may have to start by praying like this: "Lord God (if you do exist), at your word (if you really said it), I pray to you (if you can really hear me) to forgive my sin, to be with me in my fear, to comfort me in my loneliness, to show me my neighbor, to warm my heart with love, and in all the good and the hard places, the heights and the depths in my life, let me feel your hand—the hand that reaches out for me and leads me, the hand that lifts my burdens, that smooths the troubled brow and makes death easy because my head can rest in it. Tomorrow I will arise and trade with my pounds for you and serve my neighbor as if you really existed. Then you will break through the great silence that surrounds you and suddenly you will be with me."

That's the way it is with God: when we listen God speaks, when we obey God acts. "Him who comes to me I will not cast out" (John 6:37, RSV), says Jesus Christ. And for this word he died. So seriously did he take us. He deserves that we give him a chance.

## 65. What Is Your Life?

### T. DeWitt Talmage

•

What is your life? JAMES 4:14

I. *Our life is a test.* Men, angels, and devils are finding out what is in you, what you are worth, and what your weaknesses are. No man liveth to himself. Every word you speak, every action you perform, has a thousand echoes. Earth, and heaven, and hell are gazing on your behavior, and you are on trial. You are watching me, to see whether I am faithful or unfaithful; I am watching you, to see whether you are faithful or unfaithful; and each one of us is going now through the solemn, unmistakable, tremendous test.

II. *Our life is an apprenticeship.* We do not work in this world; we are only getting ready to work. We are apprentices, and have not served our time out. We are students, and have not got our diplomas. Death is to be graduation. It will be commencement day.

III. *Our life is a conflict.* If you have attempted to live a holy life, and to be better and to do better, then you sympathize with the Apostle Paul when he represented our life on earth as a war with the world, a war with the flesh, a war with the devil. In addition to the struggle you have within, you have had a thousand outside battles.

IV. *Our life on earth is a prophecy.* By that I mean that what we are in this world we will be in the world to come, only on a larger scale. I know sometimes there are marvelous changes in the last hour of life, and that the dying thief, repenting, goes to paradise; but that is the exception. The probability is that what you are in the present you will be in the future—what you now are you will always be, only with wider range.

V. *Our life is a preparation.* If we are going on a long journey, we want some time to get ready. God has started us on a journey that will have no terminus, and, once started, we never come back. Are we getting ready? If you have any lamps to light, you had better light them now.

VI. *Our life is a great uncertainty.* Nobody steps out of life as he expects to. We can make no calculation about the future. We resolve on one thing, we do another. Our associations change. Our plans change. We change. And life is such a complete uncertainty that I would not want to live one hour without the grace of God, and I very certainly would not want to die without it. Blessed be God, I feel under my feet a rock firmer than the everlasting hills. That keeps me hopeful and confident. No overbearing autocrat sits on the throne of the universe. My Father is king; and the mountains may depart, and the hills be removed, but his goodness, and his kindness, and his grace, never, never.

## 66. Our Part in Our Salvation

ARTHUR JOHN GOSSIP

> Indeed the whole of the crowd made efforts to touch him, for power issued from him and cured everybody. LUKE 6:19, MOFFATT

If we are really to reach Christ, we too will need to struggle to get near him.

For one thing, it is not easy—is it?—to believe that he can really help us? Once it was possible, perhaps, but it's not likely now. Our ways are so set, our habits are so fixed, we have become so accustomed to be this we are, and it no longer hurts us much. In any case, for good and evil, this is actually what we are, and we don't look for any marked change now. And accordingly the great news of the Gospel blows somewhat idly through our mind. We don't challenge its truth, nor doubt it in the least. For we have seen it working out in other lives. But we are not surprised that it seems to do little in our case. We never really thought it would. How can it, with our characters so gnarled and strong?

Or our past failures have disheartened us. For how often at a communion, or elsewhere, we have been really moved, and swore hot vows of very definite amendment. And then somehow it dropped out of our mind, and we slipped back into the customary ways; and so time after time it fizzled out in a mere resultless emotion.

And you and I may have to struggle too, through apathy

and doubt, and a sordid contentment with things as they are, and many another hindrance. Still push you in, like that blind man refusing to be silenced, crying and crying out there on the far edge of the crowd—a perfectly hopeless position, you and I would have said—and elbowing a way where there was no way, nearer and nearer Christ: or like that woman, caught there in the press, and swept helplessly to and fro by its surging rushes, now with her hope alight, for she had almost reached him, now tossed away from him again, until at length, wedged tightly as she was, she just managed, as once more she was carried past, to touch him with her fingertips. Struggle you, too, to him; touch him like that, and to you also there will come that healing you must have, that new power for which you have yearned in vain so long; and you, too, will become another creature, with another higher, fuller, happier, healthier life. But you must fight your way to him, must really believe that he can really help you.

Still it is difficult—is it not so?—for us who know it all so well to raise faith to the temperature at which it works and grows really effective; to keep on believing with any vividness of expectation; to avoid slipping into nothing more purposeful than a vague feeling that in some undefined way something, perhaps, may come of it in the end, sometime, by and by. That is not nearly enough to bring things to the point, and to create the atmosphere in which Christ's power can work.

There is a verse into which there are crowded in one splendid constellation the three most characteristic words of the New Testament: "By grace are ye saved through faith" (Eph. 2:8). That is to say, there is a Giver, an amazing Giver, prodigal in his lavish generosity, who gives his best to anyone for nothing. There is a gift, how glorious a gift (for what can anybody need that there is not in Jesus Christ, our marvelous Savior?). But there must be also hands outstretched—is not that what faith means?—lean, empty, eager hands willing to take, and wistful to receive. It is that last that fails.

Well, if things are ever to right themselves, this bold and valorous appropriating faith must begin in some heart. And why should it not be in yours and mine? Think, think until it all grows vivid to your heart again; stand still on Calvary and look until you see it; struggle toward Jesus Christ, through everything that dims and dulls the Gospel to you, until you have that ardent, watchful eagerness of faith that comes into his presence with a happy sense that great things are upon the threshold, and that sees doors opening to let in who knows what? For who can reckon up what Christ can do? It is so small a part in our salvation he has left to us! But if we did it, what would we not see? Why not begin to give him, here and now, that happy expectancy that normally he needs in us, so that for us too, for each one of us, it may all come wholly true.

## 67. Finding Stability in a Changing World

C. Adrian Heaton

•

Scripture: Psalm 46

In this age of tranquilizers it is more and more apparent that neither Congress, nor Social Security, nor the United Nations can really guarantee us freedom from fear. We are tortured by ill health, highway catastrophe, moral corruption, job insecurity, and the breakdown of our homes and churches. In a world like this, are peace and security even remotely possible? The Psalmist declares, "God is our refuge and strength, a very present help in trouble. Therefore we will not fear" (Ps. 46:1-2).

This psalm, probably written to mark the victory in Jerusalem over the aggressive forces of Sennacherib, proclaims the power of God. The words of this psalm have through the centuries been an encouragement to all of God's people who must face trial and hardship.

I. *The Changing World.* In verses 2 and 3 the poet describes the world in transition. The earth is "changed," the mountains "shake into the heart of the sea," "the waters roar and foam," and there is a great "tumult." Other Biblical pictures remind us that the unbeliever is like "chaff which the wind drives away" (Ps. 1:4, RSV), or like one who builds his house upon the sand (*see* Matt. 7:24-27). Our unbelieving world is crumbling and falling. Newspaper headlines report violence and death, kingdoms and empires totter, and war clouds hang low. Such human predicaments magnify the faithfulness of God.

II. *The Changeless God.* Our God is described as a "refuge and strength." He is the same yesterday, today, and forever. Through the ages he has been offering his grace and mercy to penitents and his just judgment upon impenitents.

But more than all else, the central affirmation of the psalm is that this dependable God is a very *present* help. Occasionally, a friend will wish to brace up my spirits by saying, "Cheer up, old chap, the first hundred years are the hardest." But such words do not really cheer me, for it is the first hundred years that I am troubled with. The Scriptures, on the other hand, tell me God is a present, not a far-off help.

Verse 4 speaks of "a river" which "makes glad the city of God." Historians of the ancient world tell us cities grew in size and influence only when they were situated on a seacoast or on a river. Water is essential for irrigation, purification, transportation, and protection. Yet Jerusalem, a totally inland city, became a great city, for as the Psalmist reminds us, God himself is the fountainhead of purification, protection, nourishment, and all that in the natural world is provided by water. Verse 5 makes this clear: "God is in the midst of her."

The concept of the river flowing through the city of God is transformed in the New Testament to "the water of life" within the heart. Jesus spoke of this to the woman at the well (*see* John 4:7-15).

A witness to the nearness of God is found in verses 7 and 11.

The words "The Lord of hosts is with us" in the original are *Jehovah sabbaoth emmanu.* Here is the name of God, Jehovah of hosts, in his saving relationship with his people. The last word *emmanu* is the prepositional phrase "with us." You will recognize that one of the names of Jesus is Emmanuel. The "el" ending refers to God. Those who know Jesus Christ and live in fellowship with him have God present in their lives. No wonder the Psalmist and the Christian say, "Therefore we will not fear."

III. *The Changed Believers.* Christ invites those who were once a part of the changing, fickle, and transitory world to become stable, secure, and permanent as through him they learn to trust God. We who were once "like the chaff which the wind driveth away" may become like "the tree planted by the rivers of water." We who once were like the man who built his house upon the sand may now be like the man who builds his house upon the rock. When we confidently trust in Christ, the changing world will not unsettle us.

# 68. The Thirst for Life

### EDWARD W. STIMSON

●

> Jesus answered her, "If you knew the gift of God, and who it is that is saying to you, 'Give me a drink,' you would have asked him, and he would have given you living water." JOHN 4:10, RSV

The refrain of a once-popular song is "I love life, I love life, *I love life!*" Most people love life, although not necessarily as it is, but as they hope it may become. They admit that there is more to life than they have found and enjoyed. Many people, like a weary man in a parched land, yearn for refreshment from a deep, cool spring.

Jesus apparently was thirsty when he asked for a drink from that woman who had come at midday to draw water from the well in Samaria. When she expressed surprise that he, a Jew, would make such a request of a Samaritan woman, Jesus said, "If you knew the gift of God, and who it is that is saying to you, 'Give me a drink,' you would have asked him, and he would have given you living water."

A social outcaste and ostracized by the other women of Sychar, that unnamed woman had come to draw water at this hot, inconvenient time so that she might avoid the snubs and slights of her censorious neighbors. Yet Jesus not only spoke to her but also asked a favor—a drink from her water jar. The Lord of life, who thought of no person as being beyond the claim of God's love, knew that there was goodness in her. He invited her to be generous in a way that was within her immediate capability.

Preaching on this text to a congregation which included a number of refugees in the Drum Tower Church in Peking several years ago, I pressed the Gospel teaching that no one is worthless to Christ. I emphasized that he sees hidden and latent possibilities in even the most unlikely persons and asks them to serve his kingdom. After the service a Chinese refugee said that she had contemplated suicide, but that now, having found the Christ who loved her and expected her to serve him by giving a drink of water to others in need, the fountains of joy in her heart had been opened.

The woman of Samaria was too dull-witted to comprehend what Jesus meant when he said that she should ask for living water. "The well is deep," she said; "where do you get that living water?" When Jesus tried to help her to understand by saying that whoever drank of the water he offered would never thirst again, she exclaimed, "Sir, give me this water, that I may not thirst, nor come here to draw."

Then, gently and patiently, Jesus broached the moral problem in her life which prevented true spiritual refreshment. He asked her to call her husband. Then he complimented her for her honesty when she said, "I have no husband," because though she had had five husbands, she was not married to her present companion.

When she attempted to change the course of the conversation to the sectarian differences between Jews and Samaritans, he brought her thinking once more to spiritual sustenance by saying that God is Spirit and all true worshipers must worship him in spirit and in truth. He required that she look into her own spirit and face the truth of her life before God.

Here is insight into the difficulty of many a modern soul. The thirst for life cannot be satisfied by gratifying our lower passions or in the pursuit of wealth, popularity, or fame. Life at levels less than that of the Spirit will not quench our higher thirst. That will come only as we drink at the fountain of living water which Christ provides. His forgiving grace cleanses away the debris that clogs our inner wells and permits his spirit of truth and loving goodness to flow within our hearts.

> I heard the voice of Jesus say,
>     "Behold, I freely give
> The living water, thirsty one,
>     Stoop down, and drink, and live."
> I came to Jesus and I drank
>     Of that life-giving stream;
> My thirst was quenched, my soul revived,
>     And now I live in him.

# 69. The Birthright of the Godly

Philemon F. Sturges

•

Which were born, not of blood, nor of the will of the flesh, nor of the will of man, but of God. John 1:13

Embedded in the majestic prologue to the Fourth Gospel stands this phrase: "which were born, not of blood, nor of the will of the flesh, nor of the will of man, but of God." The writer is prefacing his Gospel with the question of the origin of things. "In the beginning." Before he takes up his exposition of the life of Jesus, he dogmatizes on ultimate questions.

You may think that you have no theology nor care to have one, you may indeed resent dogma, you may think that after all the theologies and systems of metaphysic have had their say, the thing that makes a difference to life is what a man does and not what a man believes. But sooner or later, in one way or another, you face and answer the very questions with which this prologue to the Fourth Gospel is dealing. Who are you? What are you here for? Whence do you come? What is the determining principle on which your being and your thinking rest?

Consciously or unconsciously, into the choices and aims of your everyday business of living there enters inevitably the consideration of what you believe you are. And the question as to what you believe you are born of is an immediate question to the way you see your life. Central to the teaching of Jesus is the doctrine of your parentage. And at the very outset of the Gospel that attempts to interpret the mind of Jesus is this affirmation that you were born of God. "Not of blood, nor of the will of the flesh, but of God." It is, so to speak, the major presupposition from which all Christian thought about our nature and our way of living takes its start.

# 70. The Courage Christ Instills in Men

CHARLES FISKE

•

And they were in the way going up to Jerusalem; and Jesus went before them. MARK 10:32

The appeal of Calvary comes to us out of this splendid courage of the Master. With us it is so natural to choose easy roads. Here is One who wins our admiration and allegiance because he stood every test and was ready to endure every strain at the call of duty—quick always to do the right thing, even though it be the hard thing, never swerving a hair's breadth in his purpose or allegiance, walking fearlessly in the way of truth and right when he knew that it could but lead to Calvary and the Cross.

I shall never forget a sermon I heard long ago in college days in which the preacher repeated again and again the sentence, "Jesus Christ did not come into the world to make life easy; he came to make men great." That was the wonderful truth the first followers of Jesus learned from their Master, that while this may be a hard world in which to be perfectly happy, it is a great world in which to build character. The secret of all sin is to choose the easy way, to hold back and save oneself from sacrifice. The secret of all life is to press forward toward the right, however much it may cost and however much it may hurt. The spirit of Christ is always a challenge to the heroic.

And yet we are so afraid to accept the challenge for ourselves or to present it to others. That is why our modern Christianity fails so often in its appeal to youth. We take our religion so easily; we allow it to evaporate into a dead, dull respectability; we are so unready to put ourselves to any serious inconvenience for the things in which we are supposed to have faith; we are slaves to our surroundings, swept along in the current. Even when we attempt to stand against what we know to be wrong, our effort is poor and paltry, a mere apology for courage; we insinuate a feeble effort which is quickly swept aside, and we then slip back, hardly leaving a dent on any man's conscience, so weak have been our blows.

It is the heroic Christ on the Cross who draws us to himself. Think of him as he won the penitent thief. Here, probably, was a youth who had been captivated by some bold and daring spirit among the insurrectionist bands who robbed the rich for the benefit of the poor, as early first-century Robin Hoods of the Jerusalem Road. Now the man saw a leader of courage and magnanimity who could inspire his moral respect, largehearted as well as brave—and he capitulated to Christ.

Jesus Christ was great in every moment of his life; great in courage when he went into the temple and drove out the petty grafters who were turning the house of the Lord into a den of thieves; great in his denunciation of the scribes and Pharisees; great when he ventured to propound a Gospel which, though it was the fulfillment of the Law, was thought to be subversive of it; great when he faced his enemies in the synagogue; great when he set his face toward Jerusalem; great in the dignity with which he answered those who tried to trap him with clever questions; great when he went through the agony of Gethsemane without flinching from his moral purpose; great as he stood before Pilate and the Sanhedrin; so great on the Cross that the thief recognized his real royalty and the centurion in charge of the soldiers who executed him acknowledged, "Truly this was the Son of God" (Matt. 27:54).

His early followers, timid at first, became men of like courage. Their most outstanding characteristics were fearlessness, self-forgetfulness, a bravery which came from utter lack of self-consciousness in face of their conviction that they had a message and a mission to the world which they were compelled to proclaim and did declare with all the enthusiasm of new discoverers. They believed that Christ crucified was the key to the world's highest well-being, and they dared to preach their belief, though it was foolishness to some and a stumbling block to others. What did it matter to them that persecution, imprisonment, and death awaited them, if only they could preach the Gospel that would change the world?

## 71. Have You Learned to Say "Yes"?

FREDERICK B. SPEAKMAN

● 

The divine "yes" has at last sounded in him, for in him is the "yes" that affirms all the promises of God. 2 CORINTHIANS 1:20, MOFFATT

There is the peculiar Christian danger that you and I get the impression, and, in turn, give the impression, that Christianity's big business is to teach us how to say "No" to temptation. And that isn't its big concern. That is a by-product. Christianity's big concern is to enable us to say "Yes" to life. Of course, it keeps saying "No" to many things we keep wanting to do. But Christianity never says "No," except as a reflection of a higher "Yes!" Time and again in history, or in our present human relationships, it becomes the task of faith to put up "No Trespassing" signs on certain of life's values, to take certain of our habits, our actions, and insist that they must stop! But it is always because faith knows of a higher good, a nobler goal to be gained, by changing certain behavior. Christianity never says "No" except when it is certain of a higher "Yes!"

For because of its God our faith is a declaration of undismayable faith in life. And, above everything else, it is saying to you and me, You, the real you, had a spiritual origin. You right now have endless and glorious possibilities. Whatever your lot, you can go from here and find accomplishments with everlasting meaning. For you and your God today are carving away at an eternal destiny!

Quit moaning so much about sin, once said Augustine; get hold of what faith is all about and then do as you please. For if you will really let Christ in he will see to it that you will more and more please to do it his way.

The stature of our faith does not come from its commandments, once said Newton. The big thing about it is its proof that eye hath not seen, ear hath not heard, neither hath it entered into the heart of man to dream a dream too fair for God to fulfill. I am not interested in being good, snapped Paul Scherer once. Who wants to be everlastingly preening his virtues and weeding his vices? What I want to do is to stand with God against some darkness and watch some light appear. And Christ has taught me how. All the leaves of the New Testament are rustling with the rumor of it, urged C. S. Lewis. It is no mere list of negatives but that resounding affirmation that because of Christ any one of us who chooses may so live as to delight God, not just be pitied by him, as an artist delights in his work or a Father delights in his Son. Far more important for you and your world than anything you have learned to say "No" to is the deeper query, Are you learning to say "Yes" to that?

## 72. Talking to Yourself

CLIFFORD ANSGAR NELSON

•

When he came to himself, he said. . . . LUKE 15:17

What do you say when you talk to yourself? Continually a conversation goes on within yourself that is most important and significant for your spiritual health. What do you say to yourself concerning your inner ideals and ambitions, your ideas of success and failure, and about right and wrong?

The story of the Prodigal Son contains a conversation that a young man had with himself when he was in the far country. When he was caught up in the gaiety, glamor, and fun of spending his money in riotous living, he did not take time to talk with himself. He had no inclination to do this, for he was too fully absorbed in having what he considered to be a good time.

But then circumstances changed, and life no longer amused him. The romance was gone. He was alone and deserted by his friends. He has spent all and nothing was left except shame, hunger, and bad memories of what he had thought would be a glorious period of unrestrained freedom. He had, he was now ready to admit, made a mess of his life and opportunities. And he began to see himself and his life for what they really were.

At this point he began to talk seriously to himself. The story that Jesus told of this young man's conversation with himself is one of the most significant records of a soul-searching and transforming conversation any person ever experienced. He came to himself. "He came to" is the way we sometimes express the moment when an individual comes out of a trauma or trance of unreality. He came to his senses. He realized that it was not his real self that he had lived and acted. He was not made for the kind of existence that he had chosen for himself.

He talked with himself about the life he now was living. It was all wrong. He did not need to continue to feed swine. He was destined for better things. At home in his father's house the servants fared better than he in this distant place. His frank self-appraisal marked the turning point in the prodigal's career. He said to himself, "I will arise and go to my father, and will say to him, Father, I have sinned against heaven, and before thee, and am no more worthy to be called thy son: make me as one of thy hired servants" (Luke 15:18-19).

Childhood memories stirred within him, and he remembered

his home and determined to return. That was the redeeming thing. He had not completely lost his self-respect. He had not altogether forgotten the love of his father. He might have been fearful that his father would disown him and be angry with him. He might have turned to chagrin and despair.

Jesus tells the story in such a way that we know it is good to talk with ourselves in this manner. God will never forsake us nor forget us. God waits for us to "come to" ourselves, and is willing to meet us with the joy of welcome when we are ready to start life anew.

Perhaps it is time for each of us to talk to himself. The capacity for self-analysis and our willingness honestly to judge ourselves with a critical eye are evidences of genuine nobility. We must never lose our capacity to grow in self-knowledge. We so dodge, evade, and construct defense mechanisms rather than face ourselves with honest self-criticism that we become lost behind our own shadow.

Must we not learn to talk with ourselves, saying, "I am God's child. He wants me at home. He has given me an inheritance so large that all my life I can still be of use to him. Even now he will make my life count for good. I have failed him, but he will never forsake me."

Do not be afraid to talk to yourself. To do so may bring spiritual health. To know that you are lost without God may be the best indication of your soundness of spirit.

Talk to yourself candidly and with sincerity. Then turn to God, speaking the words which will assure you fullness of life: "I will arise and go to my Father."

## 73. The Pattern in the Mount

PHILLIPS BROOKS

•

> See . . . that thou make all things according to the pattern shewed to thee in the mount. HEBREWS 8:5

All kinds of men have found their ideals in Jesus. Entering into him, the timid soul has seen a vision of itself all clothed in bravery, and known in an instant that to be brave and not to be cowardly was its proper life. The missionary toiling in the savage island, and thinking his whole life a failure, has gone apart some night into his hut and climbed up into Christ, and seen with perfect sureness, though with most complete amazement, that God counted his life a great success, and so has gone out once more singing to his glorious work. Martyrs on the night before their agony; reformers hesitating at their tasks; scholars wondering whether the long self-denial would be worth their while; fathers and mothers, teachers and preachers whose work had grown monotonous and wearisome, all of these going to Christ have found themselves in him, have seen the nobleness and privilege of their hard lives, and have come out from their communion with him to live their lives as they had seen those lives in him, glorious with the perpetual sense of the privilege of duty, and worthy of the best and most faithful work which they could give.

Cannot you go to Christ today and find the idea of yourself in him? It is certainly there. In Christ's thought at this moment there is a picture of you which is perfectly distinct and separate and clear. It is not a vague blurred picture of a good man with all the special colors washed away, with nothing to distinguish it from any other good man in the town. It is a picture of you. It is you with your own temptations conquered, and your own type of goodness, different from any other man's in all the world, in all the ages, perfectly attained. If you give up your life to serving and loving Christ, one of the blessings of your consecration of yourself to him, will be, that in him there will open to you this pattern of yourself. You will see your possible self as he sees it, and then life will have but one purpose and wish for you, which will be that you may realize that idea of yourself which you have seen in him.

This, then, is the great truth of Christ. The treasury of life, your life and mine, the life of every man and every woman, however different they are from one another, they are all in him. In him there is the perfectness of every occupation: the perfect trading, the perfect housekeeping, the perfect handicraft, the perfect schoolteaching, they are all in him. In him lay the completeness of that incomplete act which you did yesterday. In him lay the possible holiness of that which you made actual sin. In him lies the absolute purity and loftiness of that worship which we have stained so with impurity and baseness. To go to him and get the perfect idea of life, and of every action of life, and then to go forth, and by his strength fulfill it, that is the New Testament conception of a strong successful life. How simple and how glorious it is!

So any moment we may turn from the poor reality to the great ideal of our own lives, which is in Christ, with one earnest question, "Lord, what wouldst thou have me to be?" We may pierce through the clouds and reach the summit, and there, seeing his vision of our possibilities, be freed at once from our brethren's tyranny, and from our own content and sluggishness, and set to work with all our might to fulfill God's image of our lives, to be all that he has shown us that it is possible for us to be, to make all things in these valley lives of ours after the pattern shewed to us in the mount.

# 74. The Victory of Faith

CHARLES KINGSLEY

•

> Whatsoever is born of God overcometh the world: and this is the victory that overcometh the world, even our faith. Who is he that overcometh the world, but he that believeth that Jesus is the Son of God? 1 JOHN 5:4-5

Do you really believe that Jesus is the Son of God? For sure I am, that if you did, and I did, really and fully believe that, we could all lead much better lives than we are leading, manful and godly, useful and honorable, truly independent and yet truly humble; fearing God and fearing nothing else. But do you believe it? Have you ever thought of all that those great words mean, "Jesus is the Son of God"?—that he who died on the Cross, and rose again for us, now sits at God's right hand, having all power given to him in heaven and earth? For, think, if we really believed that, what power it would give us to overcome the world, and all its chances and changes; all its seemingly iron laws; all its selfish struggling; all its hearsays and fashions.

I. Those chances and changes of mortal life—we should not be afraid of them, then, even if they came. For we should believe that they were not chances and changes at all, but the loving providence of our Lord and Savior, a man of the substance of his mother, born in the world, who therefore can be touched with a feeling of our infirmities, and knows our necessities before we ask, and our ignorance in asking, and orders all things for good to those who love him, and desire to copy his likeness.

II. Those stern laws and rules by which the world moves, and will move as long as it lasts—we should not be afraid of them either, as if we were mere parts of a machine forced by fate to do this thing and that, without a will of our own. For we should believe that these laws were the laws of the Lord Jesus Christ; that he had ordained them for the good of man, of man whom he so loved that he poured out his most precious blood upon the Cross for us; and therefore we should not fear them; we should only wish to learn them, that we might obey them, sure that they are the laws of life; of health and wealth, peace and safety, honor and glory in this world and in the world to come; and we should thank God whenever men of science, philosophers, clergymen, or any persons whatsoever, found out more of the laws of that good God, in whom we and all created things live and move and have our being.

III. If we believe really that Jesus is the Son of God, we should never believe that selfishness is to be the rule of our lives. One sight of Christ upon his Cross would tell us that not selfishness, but love, was the likeness of God, that not selfishness, but love, which gives up all that it may do good, was the path to honor and glory, happiness and peace.

IV. If we really believe this, we should never believe that custom and fashion ought to rule us. For we should not live by the example of someone else: but by the example of only one— of Jesus himself. We should set him before us as the rule of all our actions, and try to keep our conscience pure, not merely in the sight of men who may mistake, and do mistake, but in the sight of Jesus, the Word of God, who pierces the very thoughts and intents of the heart; and we should say daily with St. Paul, "It is a very small thing that I should be judged of you, or of man's judgment: yea, I judge not mine own self" (1 Cor. 4:3).

And so we should overcome the world. Our hearts and spirits would rise above the false shows of things, to God who has made all things; above fear and melancholy; above laziness and despair; above selfishness and covetousness; above custom and fashion; up to the everlasting truth and order, which is the mind of God; that so we might live joyfully and freely in the faith and trust that Christ is our King, Christ is our Savior,

Christ is our example, Christ is our judge; and that as long as we are loyal to him, all will be well with us in this world, and in all worlds to come.

# IX
# TEXTS THAT
# CHALLENGE

# 75. God's Love for a Sinning World

CHARLES G. FINNEY

●

> For God so loved the world, that he gave his only begotten Son, that whosoever believeth in him should not perish, but have everlasting life. JOHN 3:16

The text lays special stress on this—God *so* loved—his love was of such a nature, so wonderful and so peculiar in its character, that it led him to give up his only Son to die. More is evidently implied in this expression than simply its greatness. It is most peculiar in its character. Unless we understand this, we shall be in danger of falling into the strange mistake of those who are forever talking about God's love for sinners, but whose notions of the nature of this love never lead to repentance or to holiness. They seem to think of this love as simply good nature, and conceive of God only as a very good-natured being, whom nobody need to fear. Such notions have not the least influence toward holiness, but the very opposite. It is only when we come to understand what this love is in its nature that we feel its moral power promoting holiness.

It may be reasonably asked, If God so loved the world with a love characterized by greatness, and by greatness only, why did he not save all the world without sacrificing his Son? This question suffices to show us that there is deep meaning in this word *so,* and should put us upon a careful study of this meaning.

197

I. This love in its nature is not *complacency*—a delight in the character of the race. This could not be, for there was nothing amiable in their character. For God to have loved such a race *complacently* would have been infinitely disgraceful to himself.

II. It was not a mere *emotion* or *feeling*. It was not a blind impulse, though many seem to suppose it was. It seems to be often supposed that God acted as men do when they are borne away by strong emotion. But there could be no virtue in this. A man might give away all he is worth under such a blind impulse of feeling, and be none the more virtuous. But in saying this we do not exclude all emotion from the love of benevolence, nor from God's love for a lost world. He had emotion, but not emotion *only*. Indeed, the Bible everywhere teaches us that God's love for man, lost in his sins, was paternal —the love of a father for his offspring—in this case, for a rebellious, froward, prodigal offspring. In this love there must of course blend the deepest compassion.

III. On the part of Christ, considered as Mediator, this love was *fraternal*. "He is not ashamed to call them brethren" (Heb. 2:11). In one point of view, he is acting for brethren, and in another for children. The Father gave him up for this work and of course sympathizes in the love appropriate to its relations.

IV. This love must be altogether *disinterested,* for he had nothing to hope or to fear—no profit to make out of his children if they should be saved. Indeed, it is impossible to conceive of God as being selfish, since his love embraces all creatures and all interests according to their real value. No doubt he took delight in saving our race—why should he not? It is a great salvation in every sense, and greatly does it swell the bliss of heaven— greatly will it affect the glory and the blessedness of the Infinite God. He will eternally respect himself for love so disinterested. He knows also that all his holy creatures will eternally respect him for this work and for the love that gave it birth. But let it also be said, he knew they would not respect him for this great work unless they should see that he did it for the good of sinners.

V. This love was *zealous*—not that coldhearted state of mind which some suppose—not an abstraction, but a love deep, zealous, earnest, burning in his soul as a fire that nothing can quench.

VI. The sacrifice was a most *self-denying* one. Did it cost the Father nothing to give up his own beloved Son to suffer, and to die such a death? If this be not self-denial, what can be? Thus to give up his Son to so much suffering—is not this the noblest self-denial? The universe never could have the idea of great self-denial but for such an exemplification.

VII. This love was *particular* because it was *universal*; and also *universal* because it was *particular*. God loved each sinner in particular, and therefore loved all. Because he loved all impartially, with no respect of persons, therefore he loved each in particular.

VIII. This was a most *patient* love. How rare to find a parent so loving his child as never to be impatient. How many parents can say that you love your children so well, and with so much love, and with love so wisely controlling, that you have never felt impatient toward any of them—so that you can take them in your arms under the greatest provocations and love them *down,* love them out of their sins, love them into repentance and into a filial spirit?

IX. This is a *jealous love* in the sense of being exceedingly careful lest anything should occur to injure those he loves. Just as husband and wife who truly love each other are jealous with ever wakeful jealousy over each other's welfare, seeking always to do all they can to promote each other's true interests.

This donation is already made—made in good faith—not only *promised,* but actually *made.* The promise, given long before, has been fulfilled. The Son has come, has died, has made the ransom and lives to offer it—a prepared salvation to all who will embrace it.

# 76. Behold the Lamb!

AVERY ALBERT SHAW

•

Behold the Lamb of God, which taketh away the sin of the world.
JOHN 1:29

The central thing to remember is that the Lamb was slain. He
was overcome by the beast. If he had been willing "to die in
his bed like a gentleman," men might have remembered some
of his words, but it is doubtful if many would have been interested enough to record them. We recall how few followed him
when he was alive. It was not the baby in the manger, not the
incomparable teacher, not the great example, who was to redeem the world. There is no explanation of his redeeming
power apart from the Cross.

But it was the Christ who died, whose death, seen in the
light of the resurrection, became a triumph, who was worthy
to have dominion and power and glory. And he has been
proving his conquering might down through the centuries in
and through those who keep their eyes on him.

There have been dark generations in the life of the Church
when it thought too much about hell, copied the wild beast,
and reverted to the law of the jungle. But thank God there
have not been wanting prophets to cry, "Behold the Lamb of
God, which taketh away the sin of the world." And there is a
new conscience abroad in the world, a new spirit working in
human society. There are multitudes who have been made great
by the gentleness of the Lamb, who have become his instruments in taking away the sin of the world.

How does he do it? There are not wanting those who are
sure at this point. I have many volumes in my library which
learnedly discuss the how of redemption, and no two of them
agree. But it is not so essential how he does it, is it? But that

he has done it, is doing it today, and is mighty to save tomorrow, *that* we need to know. He has power to create a revulsion against sin. There is a story told of a woman in the Southern mountains to whom for the first time the story of Jesus' life and shameful death were told. It was incredible to her that men could deal so with such a man. "Let's hope it hain't true, Mister." George Tyrell wrote, "Again and again I have been tempted to give up the struggle, but always the figure of that Strange Man hanging on the Cross sends me back to my task again."

An African convert in Bechuanaland said to a visitor, "The Cross of Christ condemns me to be a saint." I am sure that we know ways in which he has done it for us on the level of every-day experience. Have you not seen yourself in the face of a little child, and been shamed at the things you saw in your own heart, and have been given a purpose to become worthy to stand in the presence of that innocence? Have you not seen yourself in the eyes of one you have injured, perhaps in a great experience such as Paul's, or in some less blinding but no less vivid experience, and have cried, "What shall I do, Lord?" Or you have seen yourself in the trust and confidence of your fellows, and have been shamed to deep penitence and spiritual renewal, and have vowed:

> I [will] be true
> For there are those who trust me;
> I [will] be pure
> For there are those who care.

Or it may be you have been standing on the brink of hell where your feet had well nigh slipped, and you found there was "life in a look at the Crucified One." And it is not impossible that there are those here who have gone into the pit and fought with wild beasts, a losing fight, and he brought you up out of the horrible pit and miry clay and set your feet upon a rock and established your goings. "Look unto me, and be ye saved, all the ends of the earth" (Isa. 45:22), he cries today. Of a great host whom no man can number it is true, "They looked unto him, and were lightened" (Ps. 34:5).

Perhaps this seems unreal to you. It may be that in Dr. Glover's phrase you are just "a septic soul." If you have a septic body you look to your physician who injects an antiseptic, and then tells you how to live an aseptic life. But who can cure a septic soul? "Behold the Lamb of God, which taketh away the sin of the world."

## 77. Christ's Death for Us

ROBERT RAINY

•

Christ died for our sins. 1 CORINTHIANS 15:3

To those who maintain that our Lord's death was not an offering to God, but rather an impressive and instructive demonstration to man, we say that because indeed it was an offering to God, it becomes far more effectually and completely a revelation and demonstration for us. And there are two points that may here be emphasized, as bearing on our instruction and our experience.

I. In the first place, this position tends to maintain in our minds a due sense of the exceeding sinfulness of sin, and the divine wonderfulness of God's complete and eternal forgiveness. If forgiveness were lavished on sinful creatures, on the principle that no difficulty exists but our own unreadiness to receive it, the conviction of that ill-desert of our sins, which surely is one leading factor in impressing us aright with sin's enormity, might fail to hold its due place in our minds. It may be said that forgiveness is granted in connection with repentance, and that is security enough. But repentance itself, to be real, should include the recognition of the tie that binds sin to punishment. Certainly in countless instances the loving recognition of the truth that he bore our sins, and that forgiveness comes to us allied with that great sacrifice, has been very effectual to beget and sustain in the hearts of believing men that sense of sin's wrong, and of a wonderfulness in the forgiveness of it, without which forgiveness itself loses much of its value, its meaning, its due influence on the heart.

II. And so, in the second place, this faith sustains a due impression of the love of God in Christ toward sinners. A great evidence of grace and love, no doubt, shines before us in the incarnation and the gracious life of our Lord: what but love brought him among us, or sped him on that course of merciful works and words which filled his life? And so his dying, accepted as part of his experience here, is impressively gracious, even when it is not regarded as having a more special significance, and implying a heavier burden. But there is more than this in the way in which, in Scripture, the love is argued from the death. Christ "loved me, and gave himself for me" (Gal. 2:20). "Herein is love, not that we loved God, but that he loved us, and sent his Son to be the propitiation for our sins" (1 John 4:10). "Hereby perceive we the love of God, because he laid down his life for us" (1 John 3:16). For it was his death that carried him into the very heart of our burdens and disgrace, that out of the sacrifice might arise for us all kinds of deliverance and honor.

# 78. Reconciliation by Christ

## FREDERICK W. ROBERTSON

●

*And you, that were sometime alienated and enemies in your mind by wicked works, yet now hath he reconciled.* COLOSSIANS 1:21

I. The sacrifice of Christ was the voice of God proclaiming love. The Apostle tells us that Christ has reconciled us to God "in the body of his flesh through death" (Col. 1:22). We will not attempt to define what that sacrifice was—we will not philosophize upon it; for the more we philosophize the less we shall understand it. We are well content to take it as the highest exhibition and the noblest specimen of the law of our humanity—that great law, that there is no true blessedness without suffering, that every blessing we have comes through vicarious suffering. All that we have and enjoy comes from others' suffering. The life we enjoy is the result of maternal agony; our very bread is only obtained after the toil and anguish of suffering myriads; there is not one atom of the knowledge we possess now which has not, in some century of the world or other, been wrung out of Nature's secrets by the sweat of the brow or the sweat of the heart.

This is the law of our humanity, and to this our Redeemer became subject—the law of life, self-surrender, without which reconciliation was impossible. And when the mind has comprehended this, that the sacrifice of Christ was the manifestation of the love of God, then comes the happy and blessed feeling of reconciliation.

II. The Redeemer's atonement is the reconciliation of man to man. Of all the apostles, none have perceived so strongly as St. Paul that the death of Christ is the reconciliation of man to man. Take that one single expression in the Epistle to the Ephesians—"For he is our peace, who hath made both one."

Observe the imagery with which he continues, "and hath broken down the middle wall of partition" (Eph. 2:14). The veil or partition wall between the court of the Jew and Gentile was broken asunder at the crucifixion. When death had taken place, and he was no longer the Jew, but the Man, no longer bound by limitations of time, and place, and country, then he became, as it were, a Spirit in the universe, no longer narrowed to place and to century, but universal, the Savior of the Gentile as well as the Messiah of the Jew.

Therefore it was that St. Paul called the flesh of Christ a veil, and said the death of Christ was the taking down of "the middle wall of partition" between Jew and Gentile: and therefore it is by the sacrifice of Christ, and by that alone, man can be thus reconciled to man: and on no other possible basis can there be a brotherhood of the human race.

III. Man becomes by the Redeemer's atonement reconciled to himself. That self-reconciliation is necessary, because we do not readily forgive ourselves. God may have forgiven us, but we cannot forgive ourselves. You may obtain a remission of the past, but you cannot forgive yourself and get back the feeling of self-respect, unity within, rest, by sitting still and believing that God has forgiven you, and that you have nothing left to look for. Love demands a sacrifice, and only the sacrifice of Christ replies to this, answers it, satisfies it, and makes it plain. The sacrifice of Christ was suffering in love, it was surrender to the will of God. The Apostle Paul felt this: when that Spirit was with him he was reconciled to himself. He says, "I am crucified with Christ: nevertheless I live; yet not I, but Christ liveth in me" (Gal. 2:20).

IV. Through the atonement of the Redeemer, man becomes reconciled to duty. There is no discord more terrible than that between man and duty. There are few of us who fancy we have found our own places in this world; our lives, our partnerships, our professions, and our trades are not those which we should have chosen for ourselves. There is an ambition within us which sometimes makes us fancy we are fit for higher things, that we are adapted for other and better things than those to which we are called. But we turn again to the Cross of Christ, and the mystery of life becomes plain. The life and death of Christ are the reconciliation of man to the duties which he has to do.

## 79. The Blessedness of Moral Sorrow

### John A. Hutton

•

My sin is ever before me. Psalm 51:3

I believe it is not contrary to the most perfect trust in God's mercy that we should remember the sins from which he has delivered us. It will remind us rather how much we owe to God and how closely we must keep to Christ and how humbly we must walk if we are to continue in hope. For in many cases, I fear, when we forget our sins, we are really making light of them. Whereas by remembering them, the deep reality of our life comes back to us and we feel how true it is that nothing is really past with us, that we are free of our sins only in the measure that our life is hid with Christ.

Let me name certain good results, certain holy influences which come to those who continually acknowledge their transgression, who have "their sin ever before them."

I. This exercise makes us think more truly about ourselves: it reminds us of what we are.

II. A second good result or holy influence comes to those who have their sin ever before them. By this exercise they become more kindly toward others, and especially to such as have failed in this life or have made shipwreck of themselves.

III. The third good result or holy influence which comes from having our sin ever before us is that we keep near to Christ and think of him eagerly and with joy. To whom much is forgiven, the same loveth much. If our lives are kept sober by the thought of our sins, they will always be looking toward Christ with a certain entreaty and faith.

## 80. Help Thou Mine Unbelief

### G. A. STUDDERT-KENNEDY

•

Lord, I believe; help thou mine unbelief. MARK 9:24

You have rejected the divinity of Jesus up to now, perhaps, because you felt it could not be intellectually proved, by reason, and that it was a truth which reason ought to be able to prove, and you were not going to be dishonest and say you believed when you were not convinced. I say that is all the wrong order. You cannot force or kill your intellect. Of course you can't, and you must not. The point you want to start with is his perfect humanity, the question you want to ask yourself is whether you ought to be like him. Once you have fairly and squarely decided that, you have taken the first real step to prove that Jesus was divine, that his goodness is the goodness of God, which all the travail of creation was undertaken to produce, the goodness that is good enough for real brotherhood, real peace on earth and goodwill amongst men.

Of course, your temptation will be to say that the goodness of Jesus is an impossible goodness—that it never can be yours or anyone else's. You will know it is divine all right, but your temptation will be to say that it is impossible. If you reject it on these grounds—well, you know where you are, don't you? You know you are a coward who won't climb; you can't disguise yourself as an honest man who won't lie. But if you think fair and square on any big human problem, you will come to it that this impossible goodness is necessary, inevitable, if human dreams are to come true. This impossible goodness is necessary, is the very first necessity, if we are to make the better world, for the better world can be made only out of better men.

The man who wants to make the world a better, happier place will come at last to see—if he is in earnest—that his heart's desire can come true only as this higher order of goodness is spread abroad in men's lives. If a man is going to be in dead earnest he will come at last to see that it can only be built on the foundation of that sort of goodness which is in Christ. He will come to see that the weak spot in all our schemes for betterment is human nature in its ordinary, wobbly, unreliable, good and evil state, and that on that rock our dreams are bound to suffer shipwreck soon or late. When you stand there with necessity behind you and impossibility in front, when the choice is stripped of all disguise and you see that it must be "Christ or the present chaos," then you are down on rock bottom, and will cry to the Perefct Man, "Lord, I believe, help thou mine unbelief—I do believe—I want to believe in Jesus Christ, his only Son our Lord."

# 81. No One Believes Completely

## CHARLES L. ALLEN

•

Help thou mine unbelief. MARK 9:24

Many who sincerely want to believe in God find believing to be difficult. Faith never comes easily, and the only way it comes is when we begin where we can begin and go on from that point. No one believes in all of God. No man can. God is so great and we are so small that we can believe only in a part. A man said to Jesus, "Lord, I believe; help thou mine unbelief." In every person is both belief and unbelief, for no person believes completely.

At the beach I looked as far as I could see. Between me and the distant horizon was an incalculable body of water. I could scoop up a little in a child's pail. I could taste the saltiness of the ocean. I could swim in the water and be carried on the waves. But there are marvels and mysteries within those waters which no man can fathom. Yet though we do not know all that may be known, we say with assurance, "We believe in the sea."

We also say that we believe in people. We base that belief on a very limited acquaintanceship. Our families we know intimately, and our close friends we come to know more and more as our lives are interlocked with their lives. Yet how few of the billions of people on this earth do we really know? In the people we do know, however, we see love and faith, loyalty and unselfishness, goodness and integrity, and we do not need to know every man in order to say confidently, "We believe in people."

So it is in our belief in God. He is so great that we can never know him, yet he is so near that we cannot help knowing him. The Bible tells us that "God is love" (1 John 4:8). We have loved and been loved. We have seen love expressed in many ways. By seeing and feeling love, we have come to believe in it. Believing in love is believing in God. A small part of God, to be sure, but still God.

The Bible speaks of the beauty of God. Beauty is God. Not all of God, but certainly a part of him. I watch the rainbow, I gaze upon the face of a tiny violet, and, hearing the prayer of the Psalmist, "Let the beauty of the Lord our God be upon us" (90:17), I see people for whom that prayer has been answered. I have not seen all the beauty there is, but I have seen enough to know that beauty exists. Thus I know there is a God, because beauty is a part of God.

Each day we may know a little more of God. We can never know all of him, but instead of worrying about the part of

God I do not know, I say, "Lord, I believe; help thou mine unbelief."

I. For those who find it hard to believe in God, let me point out that it is even harder not to believe. I walk along the road and find a watch lying in the dust. I pick it up and look closely at its many parts which fit together and work together. The watch indicates the time of day. It has a purpose. If you were to tell me that somebody made that watch, I would believe you, but it would be very difficult for me to believe that a watch just happened to be.

When I witness the marvelous beauty of the world in which we live, it is difficult to believe in a God great enough to have created it all, but it is hard, very much harder, to believe that there was no creative mind and heart, no divine purpose which breathes throughout it all, and that it just happened to be.

II. Many sincere people find it difficult to believe in God because we live, as the poet said, in a world of sweets and sours, and we are unable to understand why a loving Father permits the pains and sorrows which blight our happiness and separate us from our loved ones.

Great minds have long attempted to understand the mystery of pain, but no final answer to our anxious questions is possible. We do know that some suffering is caused by the law-abidingness of the universe. If we break laws which God has structured into the very nature of the universe, we shall be hurt. And God has made moral laws by which we must live. When in disobedience we break these laws, we are ultimately broken by them. Are these not in fact strong reasons for believing in God?

Much of the suffering of the world is brought about because the world is constantly struggling to overcome ignorance, poverty, and the manifold limitations of this mortal existence. The fight to better ourselves is not without pain. Yet the thrust of man toward a higher, nobler, and more Christlike life is for me a convincing evidence for believing that we live within the shadow of a God who challenges, inspires, and guides us to a higher life.

And we suffer because our lives are intermeshed and inter-related with the lives of all men. We are members one of another. If someone is hurt, we too are hurt. This is a reason for believing, for our very suffering because of the suffering of others is proof of our brotherhood, and brotherhood is a proof of a fatherhood. That fatherhood is God.

III. If you were to ask, "What must I believe?" I would not argue intellectual propositions with you. Rather, I would tell you to do what the father of the afflicted child did. He talked to Jesus about his problem.

The father of that sick boy knew the meaning of a heavy heart, of disappointment, and of frustration. The presence of evil in our lives and in our world often makes faith difficult. But in this instance it was not the absence but rather the pres-ence of evil that led him to a complete faith. The path of trouble may lead to God.

That father might have stayed home and wrapped himself in a cloak of bitterness. Instead, he went to search for Christ. To concentrate on your tragedies will destroy whatever faith you have.

Christian faith is Person-centered. That Person is our Lord Jesus. Faith never becomes real until it becomes personal. Jesus offers his loving compassion and concern to you. Accept his friendship as best you understand it. Through him your belief will grow from more to more.

## 82. The Evangelical Prophet

ALEXANDER WHYTE

•

Scripture: ISAIAH 53

It was when Jerome was engaged in translating this chapter out of its original Hebrew into his western Latin, that he exclaimed in wonder and in praise, "Surely this is the chapter of a New Testament evangelist, rather than of an Old Testament prophet!" And ever since Jerome said that, Isaiah has been known in the Church as "The Evangelical Prophet." "Not only many Jews," says the New Testament scholar Johann Albrecht Bengel, "but even atheists have been converted to Jesus Christ by means of this chapter. History records the names of some of them: God alone knows the names of them all." And John Donne says that as "in the New Testament we have 'The Gospel according to Matthew,' and 'The Gospel according to Mark,' and 'The Gospel according to Luke,' and 'The Gospel according to John': so in the Old Testament we have 'The Gospel according to Isaiah.'" "The fifty-third of Isaiah reads," says Franz Delitzsch, the German theologian, "as if it had been written beneath the Cross of Calvary. This chapter is the most central chapter, the deepest and the highest chapter, in the whole of the Old Testament. The Holy Ghost has here excelled himself," says Delitzsch.

And indeed, this most wonderful chapter deserves all, and more than all, that has ever been said in admiration of it. The Old Testament believers cast their surest anchors on this Scripture. They have more anchorages than this; but this was the surest, the safest, and the most consoling anchorage of them all. There is nothing, indeed, like this chapter even in the New Testament itself: there is no other single scripture—in the whole of the Word of God—in which the sin-atoning death of the Son of God is set before the faith of a sinner as it is here. Simply nowhere else is the redeeming death of Christ set forth so clearly, so fully, so emphatically, so explicitly, so positively, so experimentally, so impossibly-to-be-disputed, and so impossibly-to-be-for-one-moment-doubted—as it is here. A sinner must have his eyes sealed up very close indeed, not to see his salvation here. He must surely have a very seared conscience, who does not flee to the Cross of Christ as it stands so open to him in this chapter.

# X
# THE TASK
# OF THE
# EVANGELIST

# 83. Our Initiative in Evangelism

RALPH M. JOHNSON

•

Follow me, and I will make you fishers of men. MATTHEW 4:19

Since the dawn of history, God has had the initiative in evangelism. His love and initiative are revealed in Christ, who came "to seek and to save that which was lost" (Luke 19:10). God did not wait for man to save himself. "He gave his only begotten Son" (John 3:16).

Jesus shared God's initiative with his disciples. "As my Father hath sent me, even so send I you" (John 20:21). The effort of disciples then and now to help others find faith is a direct consequence of the Great Commission. In evangelism only those churches and pastors who go fishing for converts get results. We can no more wait for people to come to church than a fisherman can wait for fish to jump into his boat.

Jesus' first disciples, Galilean fishermen, were urged, "Follow me, and I will make you fishers of men." That invitation is incumbent upon all who today would follow him.

I. Following Christ in our generation means to take the initiative in evangelism. A church that thinks only of itself is a failure, for the purpose of the church and the goal of the ministry are to win men for Christ. We must reach far beyond the doors of the church.

The minister who wishes to lead others in evangelism must

be an evangelist himself, but the evangelistic thrust of the church represents much more than the endeavors of the minister. All members are called upon to follow his example and summons.

The committed layman, who is apprehensive or reluctant to take the initiative, often finds help when the pastor accompanies him on his first calls. Soon, however, the layman will feel adequate to visit people alone. The results of such an apprenticeship are impressive.

II. When should laymen begin? The answer is now. It is a mistake to think that a long period of training, a college education, or a special course of study is needed.

Actually the best time to witness is immediately after one has made his decision for Christ. If the initiative is not assumed at once, a convert begins to lose his incentive and motivation, and soon his own experience dims. The pastor's responsibility to train new members in such a way that they sense the need to win others cannot be stressed too greatly.

III. We need to respect a fisherman's joy in a good catch. He tries for the limit and rejoices in both the quantity and quality of the catch. Let us broaden our evangelistic efforts and not belittle statistics, for they indicate that new followers have been found, lives changed, and Christian homes established. Although it is true that Jesus does not say that a church must be numerically successful, but rather faithful, it is likewise true that the growing congregation is a radiant testimony of faithfulness.

A normal increase is insufficient in a day when population is exploding all around us. To keep abreast of the times, every church must grow with an ever-increasing vigor. The entire membership holds the initiative in evangelism. Minister and laymen share in this challenging responsibility.

# 84. Fishers of Men

HENRY WARD BEECHER

•

*And he saith unto them, Follow me, and I will make you fishers of men.* MATTHEW 4:19

To fish well, it is necessary to study the peculiarities of fish. It is necessary to know more than the science of ichthyology. What a book can tell a man about fishes is worth knowing, but it is little that a book can do toward making a man a true fisherman. If a man is going to fish for *fish*, he must become their scholar before he becomes their master; he must go to school in the brook, to learn its ways. And to fish for men, a man must learn their nature, their prejudices, their tendencies, and their courses. A man, to catch fish, must not only know their habits, but their tastes and their resorts; he must humor them according to their different natures, and adapt his instruments to their peculiarities—providing a spear for some, a hook for others, a net for others, and baits for each one, as each one will. To sit on a bank or deck, and say to the fishes, "Here I am, authorized to command you to come to me and to bite what I give you," is just as ridiculous as it can be, even though it does resemble some ways of preaching. The Christian's business is not to stand in an appointed place and say to men, "Here am I; come up and take what I give you as you should." The Christian's business is to find out what men are, and to take them by that which they will bite at.

You must go *to* the fish. They certainly will not come to you. You must note times and seasons. You must be informed as to their caprices. You must creep sometimes, lie down sometimes, sometimes hide, sit patiently in the leafy covert at other times, and work frequently without filling your basket, and await a better time. You must study the sky, and for their food you must search all manner of insects, and everything that relates to the work in which you are engaged. The one act of catching fish must determine your whole manner.

Luke adds to the force of this figure very much. Matthew says, "Ye shall be fishers of men"; but Luke says, "Thou shalt *catch* men" (Luke 5:10). It is very well to be a fisher, but it is a great deal better to catch what you fish for.

## 85. A Passion for Winning Men

S. D. GORDON

•

Scripture: MARK 6:30-34

There is a great word used of Jesus, and by him, the word "compassion." The sight of a leprous man, or of a demon-distressed man, moved him. The great multitudes huddling together after him so pathetically, like leaderless sheep, eager, hungry, tired, always stirred him to the depths. The lone woman, bleeding her heart out through her eyes as she followed the body of her boy—he couldn't stand that at all.

And when he was so moved, he always did something. He clean forgot his own bodily needs, so absorbed did he become in the folks around him. The healing touch was quickly given, the demonized man released from his sore bonds, the disciples organized for a wider movement to help, the bread multiplied so the crowds could find something comforting between their hunger-cleaned teeth.

The sight of suffering always stirred him. The presence of a crowd seemed always to touch and arouse him peculiarly. He never learned that sort of city culture that can look unmoved on suffering or on a leaderless, helpless crowd. That word "compassion" used of him is both deep and tender in its meaning. The word, actually used under our English, means to have the bowels or heart, the seat of emotion, greatly stirred.

The kindred word "sympathy" means to have the heart yearning, literally to be suffering the same distress, to be so moved by somebody's pain or suffering within yourself the same pain too. Our plain English word "fellow-feeling" is the same in its force. Seeing the suffering of someone else so moves you that the same suffering is going on inside you that you see in them. This is the great word used so often of Jesus, and by him.

There never lived a man who had such a passion for men as Jesus. He lived to win them out of their distressed, sinful, needy lives up to a new level. He *died* to win them. His last act was dying to win men. His last word was, "Go ye and win men." And his first act when he got back home, all scarred and marred by his contact with earth, was to send down the same Spirit that swayed him those human years to live in us that we might have the same passion for winning men that he had. Aye, and the same exquisite tact in doing it that he had.

It must be a *passion,* a fire burning with the steady flame of anthracite fed by a constant stream of oil. If it be less we will be swept off our feet by the tides all around, or sucked under by their swift current. And many a splendid man today is being swept off his feet and sucked under by the tides and currents of life because no such passion as this is mooring and steadying and driving his whole life.

It must be a passion for *winning* men, not driving or dragging, but *drawing.* Not argument or coercion, but warm, winsome wooing. Today the sun up yonder is drawing up toward itself thousands of tons of water. Nobody sees it going, except perhaps in very small part. There is no noise or dust. But the water rises up irresistibly toward the sun because of the winning power in the sun for the water. It must be something like that in this higher sphere—a winsomeness in us that will win men to us and through us to the Master.

"Oh, well," someone says, "if you put the thing that way

you'll have to count me out. I'm not winsome that way." But when we allow Jesus to take possession of us he imparts his winsomeness. For the real secret of a transfigured life is a *transmitted* life. Somebody else living in us, with a capital S for that Somebody, looking out of our eyes, giving his beauty to our faces, and his winningness to our personality.

## 86. Advertising Christ

JOHN A. REDHEAD, JR.

•

Let your light so shine before men, that they may see your good works, and glorify your Father which is in heaven. MATTHEW 5:16

Anyone who keeps his eyes open knows that advertising plays an important role in American business. Although less than one hundred years old as we know it, advertising has assumed a major role in the operation of commercial affairs. And we who bear his name are by the commission of our Lord in the advertising business. "Let your light so shine before men," he says, "that they may see your good works, and glorify your Father which is in heaven."

I. The men of Madison Avenue remind us that the first requisite of a good advertisement is that it must be *seen*. That is why signs are lighted and placed higher and higher on buildings. They are held up to claim and hold attention. Lights are made to flicker because a moving object attracts our attention more quickly than does a stationary object. Yellow is the dominant color in advertisements because yellow solicits attention more readily than does any other color. An effective advertisement must be seen. So Jesus says, "Let your light so shine before men, that they may see . . ."

There are two ways by which you may hide the light that

is in you. The first is by a denial in deed of the truth you profess to believe, and the second is by failing to seem as Christian as you are. The text agrees with Madison Avenue that the first requisite of a good advertisement is that it must be seen, for men do not light a candle and put it under a bushel.

II. A second requirement of a good advertisement is that it must be *read*. Not only must it be seen, but there must be in it a certain something which will awaken sufficient interest in the person who sees it to make him wish to read further.

We have to take off our hats to the ingenious creations of these propagandists of commerce. When we read a magazine we are often so fascinated by the advertisements that we have little time left for the articles. With color, pictures, and bits of verse here and narrative there, they achieve an attractiveness which holds our attention until we have read what they have to tell us.

Some people think that there is nothing interesting about being a Christian. I remember as a boy starting to read a book entitled *The Calling of Dan Matthews*. As soon as I discovered that the hero of the story was a minister, I put the book down and did not finish it. I thought that there could be nothing interesting or heroic in the life of a minister. The general impression of the Christian life is much the same.

But years ago a metropolitan minister preached a sermon called "The Fine Art of Making Goodness Attractive," and here and there you and I have known people who possess that fine art and we thank God for them. By their "good works" their light never ceases to shine, and they are epistles "known and read of all men" (2 Cor. 3:2).

III. An advertisement must not only be seen and read, but it must possess a genuineness which will make it *believed*. It is not without reason that the most successful advertising clubs have adopted as their motto the word "Truth." Dishonesty in advertising is usually suicidal.

Our Lord loses when his followers display in their show windows values which they do not carry in stock. His life showed a perfect correspondence between creed and conduct. Had there been any discrepancy between what he professed and what he practiced, you and I would know nothing about him today. "The Word was made flesh, and dwelt among us, (and we beheld his glory . . .) full of . . . truth" (John 1:14).

IV. The final requisite of a good advertisement is that it must secure decision and *get action*. Even though it is seen and read and believed, an advertisement is worthless to the advertiser until it gets action.

Salesmen know this. Their companies have written advertisements which are seen and read and believed and which carry the story they have to tell; but if these alone could do the job, then salesmen would be without jobs. The company could dispense with their services. The reason salesmen have vital positions is to win customers. Someone must see a man, invite him to make a decision, and put his name on the dotted line. It is not otherwise in our calling as Christians.

## 87. Christ's Touch

ALEXANDER MACLAREN

•

Jesus . . . put forth his hand, and touched him. MARK 1:41

"Behold the servant of the Lord" might be the motto of this Gospel, and "He went about doing good, and healing," the summing up of its facts. We have in it comparatively few of our Lord's discourses, none of his longer, and not very many of his briefer ones. It contains but four parables. This Evangelist gives no miraculous birth as in Matthew, no angels adoring there as in Luke, no gazing into the secrets of Eternity, where the Word, who afterward became flesh, dwelt in the bosom of the Father, as in John. He begins with a brief reference to the forerunner, and then plunges into the story of Christ's life of service to man, and service for God.

In carrying out his conception the Evangelist omits many things found in the other Gospels, which involve the idea of dignity and dominion, while he adds to the incidents which he has in common with them not a few fine and subtle touches to heighten the impression of our Lord's toil and eagerness in his patient loving service. Perhaps it may be an instance of this that we find more prominence given to our Lord's touch as connected with his miracles than in the other Gospels, or perhaps it may merely be an instance of the vivid portraiture, the result of a keen eye for externals, which is so marked a characteristic of this Gospel. Whatever the reason, the fact is plain, that Mark delights to dwell on Christ's touch.

First, he puts out his hand, and "lifts up" Peter's wife's mother, and immediately the fever left her (1:31); then, unrepelled by the foul disease, he lays his pure hand upon the leper, and the living mass of corruption is healed (1:41); again, he lays his hand on the clammy marble of the dead child's forehead, and she lives (5:41). Further, we have an incidental statement that he was so hindered in his mighty works by unbelief that he could only lay his hands on a few sick folk and heal them (6:5). We find next two remarkable incidents, peculiar to Mark, both like each other and unlike our Lord's other miracles. One is the gradual healing of that deaf-and-dumb man whom Christ took apart from the crowd, laid his hands on him, thrust his fingers into his ears as if he would clear some impediment, touched his tongue with saliva, said to him, "Be opened"; and the man can hear (7:34). And the other is, the gradual healing of a blind man whom our Lord again leads apart from the crowd, takes by the hand, lays his own kind hands upon the poor sightless eyeballs, and with singular slowness of progress effects a cure, not by a leap and a bound as he generally does, but by steps and stages; tries it once and finds partial success, has to apply the curative process again and then the man can see (8:23). In addition to these instances there are two other incidents which may also be adduced. It is Mark alone who records for us the fact that he took little children in his arms, and blessed them. It is Mark alone who records for us the fact that when he came down from the Mount of Transfiguration he laid his hand upon the demoniac boy, writhing in the grip of his tormentor, and lifted him up.

There is much taught us, if we will patiently consider it, by that touch of Christ's, and I wish to try to bring out its meaning and power.

I.  Whatever diviner and sacreder aspect there may be in these incidents, the first thing, and in some senses the most precious thing, in them, is that they are the natural expression of a truly human tenderness and compassion.

II.  And now take another point of view from which we may regard this touch of Christ: namely, as the medium of his miraculous power.

III.  Consider Christ's touch as a shadow and symbol of the very heart of his work. Christ's touch had much significance, if we remember that, according to the Mosaic legislation, the priest and the priest alone was to lay his hands on the tainted skin and pronounce the leper whole. So Christ's touch was a priest's touch. He lays his hand on corruption and is not tainted. The corruption with which he comes in contact becomes purity. Are not these really the profoundest truths as to his whole work in the world? What is it all but laying hold of the leper and the outcast and the dead—his sympathy leading to his identification of himself with us in our weakness and misery?

IV.  Finally, we may look upon these incidents as being in a very important sense a pattern for us. Lay your hands on the sinful as Christ did, and they shall recover. All your holiness and hope come from Christ's laying hold of you. Keep hold of him, and make his great pity and loving identification of himself with the world of sinners and sufferers your pattern as well as your hope, and your touch, too, will have virtue. Keeping hold of him who has taken hold of us, you, too, may be able to say, "Ephphatha . . . be opened," or to lay your hand on the leper and he shall be cleansed.

## 88. The Community of Deferred Hopes

### H. GUY MOORE

●

One man was there, who had been ill for thirty-eight years. When Jesus saw him and knew that he had been lying there a long time, he said to him, "Do you want to be healed?" The sick man answered him, "Sir, I have no man to put me into the pool when the water is troubled, and while I am going another steps down before me." JOHN 5:5-7, RSV

This famous pool at Bethesda is a wretched sight, the gathering place for the city's sick, the invalids, blind, lame, paralyzed: the helpless, hopeless, and many of them, friendless.

We are not surprised to find Jesus there. It was like him to be in such a place. As he looks upon that crowd of suffering humanity, one man in particular attracts his attention. "There," someone may have pointed out to him, "is a hopeless case if ever I saw one!"

For thirty-eight years an illness has laid hold upon his life. He is only one among a whole multitude of discarded and all-but-forgotten men and women. Yet, he along with those who shared his burden clung to one fragile hope—a blind superstition that in the bubbling waters of that ancient pool he might be healed. But for thirty-eight years that hope had been deferred.

I. His plight reminds us that after nineteen centuries of the compassion and mercy of Christ we still live in the communities of deferred hopes. General Carlos Romulo, speaking before a world conference, said, "We belong to the community of the hurt, the heartbroken, and of deferred hopes."

Who are they? Where do they live? Of course, the answer is,

"All over the world." But "all over the world" includes my community and yours. Among them are the blighted, sad, and broken lives of every community—the "lower end" of every Main Street, the winoes, alcoholics, dope addicts, and prostitutes.

And there are the disinherited of every community, those who, perhaps through no fault of their own, are without the opportunity or strength of will to make life different from what it is. They are the racial minorities in an inhospitable society, the economically underprivileged, the uneducated and illiterate. They are denied the privilege of being accepted as human beings in a fluent, busy, and unconcerned society.

But these represent only a part of those who have become the victims of hopes deferred. Others come from all walks of life. Behind the façade of wealth, education, and social status live those for whom life has come to little or nothing at all. They do not live by the Spirit of Christ nor within the Will of God. They do not live for their fellow men or the glory of God. Their religion, even though they maintain "respectability" by belonging to the right church, is a kind of disconnected superstition consisting of the bits of knowledge that they have picked up here and there.

So "deferred hope" is no respecter of persons. It is a part of the very existence of the empty and the forgotten, and those for whom life has lost its meaning and purpose. These are they who have never encountered Christ personally. And even more tragic is the fact that we have never brought the lost man and Christ together.

II. That community of suffering about the pool within the confines of Jerusalem says something about Jerusalem and about a religion whose temple cast its shadow across Bethesda but whose leaders cared more about "keeping the Sabbath" than they did in helping a man who had been sick for thirty-eight years.

The presence of the people of deferred hopes in our communities says something about us. Do they really belong to us? Do we in any way share in their lostness, hurt, brokenhearted-ness, and deferred hopes? Are our consciences Christian enough for self-identity, compassion, and sympathy? Walt Whitman wrote:

> Agonies are one of my changes of garments,
> I do not ask the wounded person how he feels,
> I myself become the wounded person.

Of all the forces in a community the church, "the fellowship of the concerned," should feel the burden of those who are lost and seek to do something for them. But you say, "Our church does care," and indeed it does. We are grateful for our broad and comprehensive mission ministry. To some degree, at least, we participate in the healing, teaching, and saving ministry of the Lord Christ all around the world. For this opportunity and the extent we share in it we are grateful.

This must never excuse us from accepting personal concern and responsibility. The most tragic indictment that could ever be leveled against us are the tragic words of this lonely and forgotten man: "Sir, I have no man to put me into the pool when the water is troubled, and while I am going another steps down before me."

III. But for our Lord, man's hopes might be forever deferred. The man whom no one else saw was the one man whom Jesus saw. The one whom all the rest neglected was the very man whom Jesus chose. That was like Jesus, and that is the religion of Jesus. To love the unloved, to love the loveless and befriend the friendless, is to imitate Jesus in his relations with men. When Jesus entered the scene of pitiful need at the Pool of Bethesda, a revolution was wrought in the moral history of mankind.

He never met a man who was beyond helping. He has a way of taking hold of the faintest spark of hope within us and fanning it into a flame. "Do you want to be healed?" He stands today where no one else can stand—between the mercy and grace of God and the hurt, lonely, and brokenhearted—and he gives new hope, new strength, new courage, and new life.

# SOURCES
# CONTRIBUTORS
# INDEX

# Sources

*Listing is according to sermon number.*

3  From *The Pulpit in the South* (1950), pp. 107-109.
6  *Light and Truth* (1869), pp. 96-99.
7  *The Gateways of the Stars* (1928), pp. 107-110.
9  *The Day of the Cross* (1909), pp. 249-252.
11  From *Evangelical Sermons of Our Day* (1959), pp. 301, 303-306.
12  *The Greatest Questions of the Bible and of Life* (1958), pp. 65-67.
14  *The Kingdom Is Yours* (1952), pp. 33-35.
18  *Christ and His Salvation* (1869), pp. 71, 90-92.
19  *The Cross through the Open Tomb* (1961), pp. 125-128.
20  *Not a Sparrow Falls* (1952), pp. 54-55, 61, 62.
24  *The Silences of Jesus* (n.d.), pp. 49-52.
25  *The Ladder of Christ and Other Sermons* (1912), pp. 116, 118-122.
26  *Respectable Sins* (1909), pp. 139-141, 143-144.
28  *Difficult Sayings of Jesus* (1962), pp. 116-120.
29  *National Awakening* (1936), pp. 56-58.
30  *The Face of God* (1935), pp. 36-37, 39-40, 44-46.
32  *No Escape from Life* (1958), pp. 173-175.
33  *And Judas Iscariot* (1906), pp. 96-100.
36  *A Quest for Souls* (1917), pp. 308-310, 312-314.
37  *Sermons from Revelation* (1953), pp. 153-154, 155, 156-157, 158.
39  *The Dynamite of God* (1918), pp. 287-288, 289, 290.
42  *Westminster and Other Sermons* (1888), pp. 46-49.
43  *Rainbows through the Rain* (1938), pp. 105-108.
44  *Who Goes There?* (1958), pp. 91-93.
46  *Rediscovering the Words of Faith* (1956), pp. 37-40.
48  *Beneath the Cross of Jesus* (1959), pp. 129-131.
51  *His Gifts and Promises* (n.d.), pp. 93-95.
52  *The Secret of Happiness* (1955), pp. 88 ff. (Permabook edition).
55  *Favorite Sermons* (1959), pp. 115-117.
56  *The Healing Cross* (1939), pp. 26, 29-31.
57  *The Gates of New Life* (1938), pp. 21-22, 25, 27, 29, 30-31.
58  *Design for Christian Living* (1953), pp. 87-90.
60  *The Way Everlasting* (1911), pp. 217-221.

61   *The Gift of Influence* (1908), pp. 256-259, 261-262.
63   *The Ideal Life* (1897), pp. 128-131.
64   *Christ and the Meaning of Life* (1962), pp. 165-166.
65   *Great Pulpit Masters,* Vol. VII (1951), pp. 234-238.
66   *The Galilean Accent* (1926), pp. 255, 256, 257, 262, 262-263.
69   *Our Common Loyalty* (1936), pp. 61-62.
70   *From Skepticism to Faith* (1934), pp. 104-106.
71   *The Salty Tang* (1954), pp. 87-89, 91-92.
73   *Selected Sermons* (1949), pp. 305-306.
74   *Village Sermons and Town and Country Sermons* (1891), pp. 234-236.
75   *Sermons on Gospel Themes* (1877), pp. 5-8.
76   *Life at Its Best* (1935), pp. 47-50.
77   *Sojourning with God* (1902), pp. 310-312.
78   *Sermons* (1879), pp. 771-774.
79   *The Best of John A. Hutton* (1950), pp. 97-99.
80   *The Best of Studdert-Kennedy* (1948), pp. 36-37.
82   *With Mercy and with Judgment* (n.d.), pp. 201-202.
84   *Forty-six Sermons* (n.d.), pp. 313-314.
85   *The Treasury of Quiet Talks* (1951), pp. 132-133, 135-136.
87   *The Best of Alexander Maclaren* (1949), pp. 135-136, 137, 139, 140-141.

# Contributors

*Listing is by page number.*

# Index of Biblical Texts

*Listing is by page number.*

*Format by Sidney Feinberg*
*Set in Linotype Baskerville*
*Composed, printed and bound by The Haddon Craftsmen, Inc.*
HARPER & ROW, PUBLISHERS, INCORPORATED